It has been said: 'To an idea ...
and to a theory, a different the ...
Read this book of Johannes Hartl on his journey with Jesus and try
to see if you can resist the evidence radiating from it. I could not.
This book tells us, better than many treatises on Christology, that
Jesus Christ is alive.

P. RANIERO CANTALAMESSA O.F.M. CAP.
Preacher to the Papal Household

One of my favourite worship songs of all time is Misty Edwards 'I
Will Waste my Life'. I had a radical encounter with Jesus when I
was sixteen years old, and since that day, Jesus has fully captured
my heart. I gladly give every moment of my life for God, and I will
go anywhere and do anything with him. In his book *Heart Fire*,
Johannes Hartl captures a heart of love for Jesus that led him to birth
the Augsburg House of Prayer. Johannes opens his very personal
journey searching to know God intimately in this beautiful book
about the pursuit of God through prayer. We can all learn from his
devotion and passion for the One who is worthy of it all.

HEIDI G. BAKER, PHD
Co-Founder and CEO of Iris Global

Johannes Hartl calls to the deep in us that longs to know the fire
within – inspiring us to pursue prayer more passionately, and
therefore know God more intimately and to see his power more
fully. His book gives us vision to encounter Jesus more consistently
and to live in wonder of a life dedicated to prayer.

MIKE BICKLE
Director, International House of Prayer of Kansas City

An exhilarating and poetic immersion into the eternal call of God to the heart of every person. Intimacy with God is where we truly discover who we are and from which all fruitfulness comes. Johannes Hartl knows who he is and I have witnessed, first hand, the fruit that has flowed from his and his community's answer to the call of prayer.

FATHER JAMES MALLON
Priest and Author

Absolutely brilliant book! I love the radical and authentic journey Johannes has been on and it is still unfolding! The stories in this book will inspire many to wholly pursue the Lord on an entirely new level as well as seek greater depths in prayer. He and the Augsburg House of Prayer are bright and shining lamps in Europe that are also visible here in America. His work is a much-needed prototype establishing ecumenical centers of prayer and worship, ushering in renewal and revival, breaking dividing walls, and equipping and training the next generation to lead Book of Acts lifestyles.

KEITH MAJOR
Co-Founder and President of MajorChange and 'Stone to Flesh' School of the Heart in Los Angeles

Johannes Hartl welcomes us into the radical ride of a life dedicated to prayer. His honesty and creativity has illuminated my vision to what prayer can be and his thirst for beauty and brilliance draws up a new yearning in the heart of the reader. *Heart Fire* has convinced me not only of the power and splendour of living in God's gaze, but the very necessity of it. Our lives make very little sense without it. This book will challenge you to live more courageously, risk your reputation for something that's greater and bigger, and equip you with tools to keep the fire burning. I regularly found myself shouting 'wow' out loud.

PIPPA BAKER
One Hope Project

Dr Johannes Hartl, theologian and mystic, is a man ablaze with the love of God – reading this book rekindled the fire in my heart with desire for Jesus.

SIMON PONSONBY
International Author, Speaker, and Theologian at St. Aldate's Oxford, UK

This book has truly stirred my heart to pray, and I know it will yours too. Johannes paints the most beautiful picture of prayer, describing different facets through charming personal stories and remarkable testimonies. He takes you on a journey into the richness of prayer, opening up hidden gems of contemplation, silence and learning to 'see' as well as bringing alive the theology of night and day worship and the importance of unity. He draws on the incredible examples of ancient mystics as well as what God is stirring in the earth today, all interweaved with his personal journey with Jesus that challenges and inspires. This book will both soften your heart for the beauty of Jesus and spur you to seek him more.

JAMES WATERS
Director of Burn 24-7 UK

I so enjoyed reading this rich book – it stirred my soul. This is no ordinary book about prayer. *Heart Fire* takes you on a journey visiting different cultures and places, and exploring Christian traditions where God is to be found. The stories are colourful, the insight profound and Johannes' transparency invites us to keep searching for the more of God to be found in our broken world. A book to own, learn from and give away.

JANE HOLLOWAY
National Prayer Director, World Prayer Centre

'What's it all about? It's about prayer, as always. What is prayer?' So begins Johannes in the introduction to his story – a love story that on one level is a refreshingly 'easy read' yet at the same time is deeply profound. Wherever you are on your journey in prayer, this book will refresh, encourage, excite and yes, will challenge you to 'go deeper'. He goes on to say: 'I am convinced that the return to prayer, the rediscovery of prayer, is the most urgent and important concern in our twenty-first century world.' There are many signs that the western Church is rediscovering a hunger for prayer, and God will use this book to accelerate that process – and impact the destinies our nations!

ALISTAIR BARTON
Director, Pray for Scotland

Johannes has had many adventures in faith on his journey of establishing a vibrant house of prayer in the heart of Europe. He is living a life of prayer and is a man of vision and passion. He has also been a blessing to many as he has travelled and preached, including here in the UK. You will enjoy the teaching and stories in this book and find your faith in God stretched and encouraged.

REV DR WILLIAM PORTER
Beacon House of Prayer, Stoke-on-Trent, England

HEART
FIRE

HEART
FIRE

JOHANNES HARTL

Muddy
Pearl

Published in 2018 by
Muddy Pearl, Edinburgh, Scotland.
www.muddypearl.com
books@muddypearl.com

The original German edition was published as *In meinem Herzen Feuer*
Copyright © 2014 SCM R. Brockhaus in der SCM Verlagsgruppe GmbH, 58452
Witten, Germany (www.scm-brockhaus.de).

ISBN 978-1-910012-52-9

British Library Cataloguing in Publication Data
A catalogue record for this book is available from the British Library

Cover design by Jeff Miller
Typeset by David McNeill www.revocreative.co.uk

Printed in Great Britain by Bell & Bain Ltd, Glasgow

CONTENTS

FOREWORD

Johannes Hartl and I were pulled over by the police. He was driving my friend Bill, Heidi Baker (the extraordinary missionary to Mozambique) and me across Augsburg, Germany. A police car flagged us down. For a minute I wondered if Johannes might be a drug dealer. Then I remembered that he's one of the most respected leaders in the German church today. The police seemed to have a bunch of questions about his car's registration plate, or its lights, or something. 'Typical German bureaucracy,' I thought, switching tack.

We were on our way to speak to thousands of people at the annual MEHR conference. I think we were running late. The delay was inconvenient to say the least. But behind me in the car, Heidi Baker immediately began praying God's blessing on these annoying policemen. And outside Johannes was smiling, being gracious and patient and kind. At that moment I realized I was officially the least godly person in the car.

Johannes Hartl is one of the most remarkable Christian leaders I have ever met. I am so glad that his voice – already well known in his native Germany – is increasingly becoming recognized and respected in the English-speaking world too.

As you read *Heart Fire*, you'll begin to realize what a beautiful paradox this man truly is. A married monk, drawn to the solitary life of prayer, Johannes Hartl somehow gathers thousands of young people to the Augsburg House of Prayer every year. He has a razor-sharp intellect and serious academic credentials, yet he's a practitioner who cares deeply about things like the lighting in the toilets. (I kid you not!) Johannes loves and learns from ancient traditions, yet he is right at the cutting edge of cultural engagement. He is a Catholic, yet his community is truly ecumenical. He is radically committed to simplicity, yet celebratory in everything he does, from the clothes he wears to the Asian food he enjoys.

I believe that Johannes carries an important message for us at a time when the Holy Spirit is uniting Christians and calling us deeper into prayer. It's a message he conveys beautifully in this memoir-devotional. There is deep teaching (check out the chapter on *epignosis*) embedded in masterful storytelling. I particularly appreciate the way he has provided practical questions and tools for further reflection at the end of each chapter.

My prayer for you as you read *Heart Fire* is that it will become a transformative journey – equipping you to become the walking, talking House of Prayer you were designed to be – helping you become the sort of person that speaks peace to annoying police officers. May the fire that burns so beautifully within Johannes Hartl become your own all-consuming *Heart Fire* too.

PETE GREIG
24-7 Prayer International
Emmaus Rd, Guildford, UK

THE QUESTION
What is Prayer?

WHAT IT'S REALLY ALL ABOUT

Somewhere in Romania, 2012
Fields rush past and there's fire in my heart.

Forests and villages race by and I've known this fire for so long. It seems to come and go and yet it's always been there.

Was that really a donkey cart?

How am I supposed to concentrate in this car?

Anyway, back to the subject. Back to the question.

What's it all about? It's about prayer, as always. Somehow, it always ends up being about prayer. About a question that has driven me for so many years: What is prayer? Making contact with a transcendent God ... can there be such a thing, really? How does it work? How can a human being actually do this? Dare we, really? And *does* it actually work? Where does it start and where does it lead? Year after year, I find new answers, deeper answers, to these questions that have plagued me since my youth. Questions that have been answered not so much through intellectual proposition, but through encounter and experience, and, not infrequently, while travelling. Like now.

So, it's about prayer, once again.

The old car, with its worn-out suspension, bumps and lumbers over the highways of Romania. Yes, it *was* a donkey cart, loaded with pale-coloured hay. Another couple of hours and I will have to answer this very question, 'What is prayer?', in front of approximately a thousand people. Cotiso has arranged all this. Cotiso and his small family spent a year with us in the Augsburg House of Prayer, and now he's back here, in his home country, to unleash a movement of prayer and passion for God. He's sitting behind the steering wheel, driving at 70mph down winding highways through the remote Transylvanian countryside. Two more hours. My scrawled notes in my pocket. Fire in my heart. And complete astonishment over how all this came to be.

I already know how I am going to start with these one thousand people: I'll tell a story. The story is mine, as it happens, and that of my friends. And yet it is not really about me at all.

Why do I give talks? Why am I driving to Romania to speak to these people? Why me, a child of the eighties from Lower Bavaria, of all places? Why do I talk about prayer?

What gives me the authority?

Stories. Encounters and experiences drawn from the first thirty-four years of my life. Stories about the unbelievable. The fascinating. The shocking. The eccentric. The different. The enchanting. Shattering every categorization. The disturbance of the existential. The breaking-in of something that is greater than the world. A flare of the very radiance that is older than created light. The great mystery. The encounter with God. Prayer. That's what this book is about.

STORIES AND LIFE

Our lives are woven together out of the stories we tell. At first, we think these are stories about our lives. Then, in hindsight, we eventually realize that there is another story. That I am not telling the story of my life, but that someone else is playing his song on this instrument. It's his story. The ancient, great story of his love and his faithfulness that streams through my own little stories, like the colourful rays of light from a prism.

The history of God is happening now. It is not a reference book, not a scientific treatise. It is a drama and a love story, full of excitement, growth, sudden endings and unexpected changes. God reveals himself to his people in just such a story. And through these stories he continues to sing his song today. With all his major and minor chords, apparent dissonances and unexpected resolutions. His beautiful song.

THE WHOLLY OTHER

Metten, Germany, late summer 1988
Orange light breaks through the foliage of the chestnut tree and the bright midday sun takes a siesta. The humming of a bumblebee, two cars driving past. At home I listen to Michael Jackson and the Beatles. I am just coming out of school.

'The Mystical reveals itself', wrote Ludwig Wittgenstein in the penultimate point of his *Tractatus Logico-Philosophicus*.[1] 'The Mystical', in this case, would be the fact *that* the world exists. The astonishment at the fact that there is something, and not everlasting nothing, has intrigued me since my youth. As it did that noon, with my satchel on my back. Unexpectedly and abruptly, it was there, great and powerful, filling every corner of my heart: astonishment at being.

A glance at my hand: it's really there. That's really me – I am. The constant flow of time in which reality unfolds: it is, in fact, all real.

The insects are still buzzing and a car drives past now and again. I stand there for several minutes and I can hardly grasp it: there is actually something. How wonderful, how anything but self-evident! The staggering astonishment at the fact that I exist and that there is a world. It isn't something that can be understood by anyone who has not felt it themselves, but for those who have, it is then impossible to believe the myth that there is nothing but the material world.

Since then, the world has not become any less mysterious to me. Of course, I have 'studied' it. But what more, exactly, have we learned by naming natural phenomena? Do we 'know about' thunder and lightning and 'recognize' them now that we have discovered their connection to electrical charges? A monstrous error of our time: we confuse 'knowing the name of something' with 'really understanding something'. Early on, my heart was wounded by the Great Mystery, and spoiled for the dullness of this-worldly mundanity.

To one who prays, the world becomes ever deeper and God ever greater.

1 Ludwig Wittgenstien, *Tractatus Logico-Philosophicus* (Routledge & Kegan Paul, 1922: Dover reprint, 1999).

AND THIS, TOO: THE HOUSE OF PRAYER

Cistercian Abbey, Oberschönenfeld, Germany, September 2013
I am sitting here writing this book. My gaze is drawn outward by the rainy morning and to the red and gold of the little gatekeeper's house across from my window. I have never entered an abbey without feeling a frisson of reverence. 'But you're the director of the House of Prayer,' says the older nun at the gate, smiling. Yes, I am. That very House of Prayer in which there has been unceasing prayer, day and night, for almost two years to the day. Shortly before that, in the summer of 2011, I had had a short conversation with my friend Raphael. He's a musician, young father and director of our night shift. With the now-legendary sentence, 'Midnight to four: it's what I'm here for,' he volunteered to cover the hours from midnight to 4am in prayer and laid the foundation that enabled us to fill 24 hours a day, 365 days a year, with prayer.

I am filled with awe when I see that places of prayer, indeed, places of unceasing prayer, are nothing new. We are part of a great, centuries-old tradition. And yet I believe that it is precisely in our time that a new prayer movement is arising among young people. A movement of people who are on their own journeys of learning what prayer is. They go out, to learn to pray. Yes, I think that many will leave their old habits and the comfort of the mainstream in order to ask the fundamental questions anew. Who is God? How can I encounter him? What will this do?

And I bring all these questions together in one question: what is prayer?

PERFUME

I am convinced that the return to prayer, the rediscovery of prayer, is the most urgent and important concern in our twenty-first-century world. And I also believe that the radical, prophetic sign of unceasing day-and-night prayer is what we most urgently need. Such a statement sounds absurd, insane even, in light of the suffering in this world and in the face of the inequalities in our own society crying out for drastic action.

And perhaps it is absurd and insane. Nevertheless, I think that the call to 24-hour prayer is biblically sound and is founded in the history and spirituality of the church. But ultimately, the driving force of all of this for me personally is something quite different from a theological insight: it is my own sheer inability to live a normal life. Or to put it in more definitive terms: *he* captivated me with his beauty and before I knew it, I had chosen a lifestyle in which only one thing was of any importance: knowing *him* and living in *him*. Everything after that, everything that came later and which will come later still, is just the unfolding of, and continuing commentary on this mere fact: beauty encountered me, and I had to follow. Jesus, your beauty encountered me. And I have followed you ever since.

As a teenager I loved perfumes. I collected aromatic oils, perfumes and teas. I made my own mixtures and was able to enjoy the intoxicating aroma of some perfect compositions. But then I encountered another perfume: 'Pleasing is the fragrance of your perfumes … No wonder the young women love you!' says the Song of Songs (1:3–4) about Jesus. And it is true. Nothing is comparable to a direct encounter with God. His love is better than wine (Song of Songs 1:2), better than all of the pleasures of this world. To a person in love, to anyone who has encountered Jesus, this truth is not a wooden doctrinal statement but knowledge drawn from experience that has proven itself a thousand times over. Jesus, your fragrance has enthralled me.

And, just as he filled my inner world then, while I was driving down Romanian streets that evening, unable to contain my joy, so he fills me still today. I follow your fragrance, Jesus, out into the great adventure. The adventure of the journey into the mysterious land called prayer. And what is prayer, anyway? Countless experiences in numerous places around the world are painting an ever-sharper picture. And I want to tell you about these experiences here.

LIGHTNING
The Beginning of My Journey into Prayer

SHE IS RADIANT

Saulkrasti, Latvia, August 2010

She's beaming from ear to ear. She just wrote 'Jesus' in the sand with her feet. She is thirteen and her English is broken.

I will never forget this Baltic beach. There were no artificial lights, and the sea came right up to the edge of the forest. We were sitting in the sauna with the temperature over a hundred when the lenses in my glasses popped out. And then we ran out into the night. The ground turned sandy even before we were out of the trees. It was cold sand, but the darkness hit us more forcefully than the cold. The Latvian night, only a few stars illuminating the cove. The black forest opened onto the black beach and went on to the black sea. We threw ourselves into the ice-cold water. The sky and the sea dissolved together into a seamless black. It was a surreal feeling, swimming in an ice-cold non-space, in which above and below were identical.

I had been speaking about Jesus over the last few days. The first evening had been terribly cold in the old school in Riga. Stony faces. The mistrust built up over decades of Communism seemed to strike us almost physically. But then, on the second day there was hesitant laughter at some of the jokes. Some people even sang along with a few songs. And then, as I had so often been allowed to experience myself: tears. Tears of joy. Tears of pain that one finally allows oneself to feel. Simultaneous laughter and weeping. The touch of God.

Full of joy and utterly exhausted, my wife, Jutta, our little son, David, and I had returned to the village on the forested cove and were now taking a walk beside the wild, romantic sea. Above us was a spectacle of riotous colour, pink-violet-yellow as the sun sank between towers of cloud. And then we met her. Writing 'Jesus' on the beach with her thirteen-year-old feet. And smiling excitedly, as only a thirteen-year-old girl can, she told me in her middle-school English that today was the day that she had given her life to Jesus. A few years before this I had written a short book with forty spiritual reflections for forty days. At some point it got translated into Latvian. And now she stands there beaming as she shows me her copy of *Basic*. She had copied the graffiti-like illustrations from the book and taken the step suggested for each day. And today she has given her life to Jesus. At the age of thirteen. In Latvia.

Full of gratitude, astonishment and wonder, I think back to the moment when God called me ...

THE EARLY CALL

God called me at an early age. After the turbulent years of the late sixties, my parents rediscovered their faith through a Bible study group and increasingly shaped our everyday family life with elements of a spiritual life. But the real example of the lived Christian life, the real benchmark for me, was hidden behind the walls of a massive complex of buildings in our neighbourhood. I had the privilege of growing up in the shadows of the Benedictine Abbey in Metten, and it was there that I found a true model of the Christian life. Admittedly, not everything that glittered in the baroque ornamentation was sanctified gold. And yet my young heart was imprinted with a sense of the holy, of the sacred and transcendent, one that will remain with me forever. In the end it was an explosive in-breaking of beauty and joy. I later found the words to describe this as 'my conversion'. It wasn't really a conversion. It was my encounter with invincible glory.

I was fourteen and looking for fun. I had grown up in a good Catholic family, was attending a monastery school and had nothing against faith and the Church – except perhaps that everything holy was also boring and everything sinful was so fascinating.

There was something formative about the music we listened to at the time. These were the early years of Nirvana – the first time I went to a disco I heard songs from 2 Unlimited and Ace of Base. But nothing really spoke to me as deeply as the much older music of the Beatles and Cat Stevens: a whiff of revolution, the dream of a completely different life.

These things came early to me. The tendency to push boundaries and do my own thing goes back to my childhood. Smoking secretly in the woods started in primary school. At thirteen came a new group of friends and a new identity: I learned to play drums and began calling myself 'Joey'. Being different was my new life plan. It started with clothes. First came the standard 'hippie' outfit, then increasingly, the outrageous and the provocative characterized my style: multiple coloured shirts, one on top of another, crazy baggy trousers, multi-coloured Converse shoes and ridiculous hats. My buddy Stephan and I hitch-hiked around, sleeping overnight wherever we happened to be. We lied about our ages to get into bars so we could get booze, and I sneaked out of the house at night to go to parties. And of course, there were lots of girls. Drugs came into the mix early on. But the first cannabis that I was able to get my hands on was home-grown and had only the mildest effect. Other attempts to get high also proved ineffective. By the time others in my clique had fallen deeper and deeper into drugs, God had already drawn me out of it.

In spite of the immature escapades during this phase, there was a lot that pointed to the way ahead. I had decided once and for all that I was going to live a different kind of life. I wanted to be revolutionary. I wanted to disregard convention and never to let the opinions of others become my measure of things. My openness to anything new – I even began to have an interest in Eastern wisdom and Zen at the time – and to try out almost anything, already held something of the later character of a radical walk with Jesus.

At the same time, early on, something began to grow in me, a disappointment with everything 'of the world'. Waking up after a night of consuming insane amounts of alcohol and indulging the cheap attitude that characterized our treatment of girls, I began to feel increasingly empty. One of my favourite songs by the Beatles, maybe the most unconventional song they ever wrote, is the psychedelic tune 'Tomorrow Never Knows'. John Lennon sings about laying down all thoughts and surrendering to the void. The void: emptiness. Right in the middle of those driving beats, in the whirring and squealing, like the sound of thousands of screeching birds, is the voice of John Lennon, in almost a recitative tone: the void. In fact, even the funniest things Stephan and I did together, even the wild parties with girls, left me with an increasingly empty, flat aftertaste. There had to be more.

OVERWHELMED BY LOVE

It happens one summer evening. The external details are quickly recounted and sound unspectacular. Like a person who has just fallen in love talking about his first kiss. 'Well, yeah, it is a kiss. And?' But for the one who has just fallen in love, it means everything. And my 'everything' happens that evening at the Congress of the Charismatic Renewal in the Catholic Church. Not that I am glad to be there. Certainly not that I am searching for God. I'm already a Christian, though I am also, I must confess, a wilful teenager who does whatever he wants.

And on that day, I don't want to listen to anything or participate in anything. During the preaching and singing, I go outside and play Frisbee with my friend Franz-Josef. Or I just sit in the back row and assume the role of a disinterested observer. That's how it is on this evening.

They're all good-looking at least, especially the girls. Astonishingly normal. And yet they are so peculiar. Raised hands, ecstatic faces. They sing 'praise music'. And it is more out of boredom than anything else that I go to the front when the call is given. Anyone who wants to receive the Holy Spirit can go to the front and people will pray for them. Yeah, instead of just sitting around here all evening, I can go to the front and let them pray for me. Why not?

What follows will sound as unpoetic as the sentence, 'I was kissed', sounds to one who's never been in love.

What follows cuts my life into two halves. Forever.

What follows is something I cannot doubt and that I will never be able to doubt.

What follows is that of which I am a witness today:

God kisses me.

The prayer is unspectacular. A young man lays his hand on my shoulder and utters a couple of freely formulated sentences. At some point he says 'Amen'. I walk away. I take a few steps and somehow everything is different. No vision, no trip, no ecstasy. Simply a certainty that sweeps everything else away: that is the Holy Spirit. An endlessly sweet happiness in which the hours that follow are utterly subsumed. It's like being completely in love but infinitely more peaceful and so much deeper. And the absolute, total assurance that I have encountered a person. A beauty that is not of this world. I can't comprehend it. Franz-Josef experiences the same thing. We hug each other. 'That's got to be the Holy Spirit,' I manage to stammer, washed over by the greatest love that I have ever felt.

AND YET SO NEW

This experience of God was different from anything religious that I had known before. It was so new that I couldn't connect it to any of the standard responses that seemed to be expected of me. This gift was so free and unearned. It had none of the character of a heavenly reward for pious behaviour, or of Christian performance mentality. I hadn't done anything after all. It was so new, so free, so beautiful.

It was so new that I had no idea what to do to conserve this experience, indeed, since that moment I have had only one question: how can one keep this Holy Spirit forever?

Months pass …

On a lonely hill outside Peel, I stare at the seagulls circling over the wild sea surrounding the Isle of Man. Martin and I are lying down on the heath philosophizing about eternity while the wind of the Irish Sea blows about us. We buy Benson & Hedges and drink Cinzano at parties that are only growing bleaker and bleaker. The out-of-control LSD-trip of that party girl, friends sneaking out for quick scx in a cave, these things fail to erase the memory of the great beauty that has struck me. A longing remains in my heart and I cannot extinguish it. The knowledge that there is something more. The knowledge that a bolt of lightning has struck me.

Yet half a year passes before I happen to hear that one can 'give one's life to Jesus'. Yes! That's what I want to do. Maybe that's the secret.

I have never regretted the contract that I wrote in my diary while sitting in my room one Sunday afternoon: 'I surrender my life to you, wholly and completely, and in return you give me the Holy Spirit, forever, wholly and completely.' A bit bold, perhaps, but still straight from my heart.

Ultimately it was this day in November that had the most lasting, life-changing impact. It was, emotionally, less impressive than the encounter in May. But it set my life on a course that would shape it forever. Only some time later did I learn that my experience was quite normal for many people. They have an experience with God but don't know how to build on it. A conscious decision to follow Jesus and a daily prayer life, I gradually learned, are exactly the tools one needs to keep the fire in the heart burning. A fire that to this day has not gone out in me. And for which I am so grateful. That a fire which was once so small is allowed to have an impact in other countries – such as in Latvia in the life of this blonde girl. She had given her life to Jesus as well, so many years later in a very different place.

ECKES EDELKIRSCH AND THE WHORE OF BABYLON

Karlstein, Germany, December 1993
The months following my decision for Jesus are a total adventure. Things that once just bored me to tears now suddenly draw me in, while much that I had enjoyed before loses all attraction. During this time, I begin to devour the Bible, learn to play my first praise songs on the guitar and then write a few. And most of all I can't wait

to tell my friends about my new experience. When that happens, it's a bit haphazard, since I do not understand it all that well myself. At night we sit around together in the youth house and goof around – unforgettable highs from *Eckes Edelkirsch*,[2] the cool feeling that we buy only Lucky Strikes these days (only a fourteen-year-old can think these things are cool …), listening to Bad Religion and Counting Crows. But the conversations keep coming back to faith, and eventually we begin to read the Bible. I open the Revelation of St. John. I have just finished *The Lord of the Rings* and to me this appears to be the closest thing to it in terms of genre. So we sit on the floor, reading about the Whore of Babylon and understanding nothing. These are the months in which I first start wearing huge wooden crosses and Jesus T-shirts (although this didn't really make my attire any more provocative than before). Gradually, four of my best friends surrender their lives to Jesus. We start a prayer group and write each other dozens of notes during class in which the main topic is increasingly Jesus and only Jesus. I begin to dream about what it would look like if we could fill the movie auditorium in our school with young people who have encountered God just as radically as we have.

It is all so new, so fresh, so alive. It seems to have very little to do with anything I previously associated with faith. It takes me a couple of years to really start to grasp what treasures had already been given to me, long before.

2 A German liqueur.

STOKING THE FIRE

There is a gigantic difference between knowing someone and being in love with someone. To the one in love, suddenly everything about the beloved seems especially radiant. This seems to describe well the change in heart of someone who sort of believes in God and then comes to know Jesus personally.

What does your personal spiritual life look like? Is it a family tradition for you, like it was for me? Have you ever made a conscious decision for Jesus? Or could it be about time to renew a decision like that? Take a minute, put down this book, and start talking to God. You can ask him to touch your heart anew, to show himself to you. You can even consciously give your worries, cares and wishes over to him. If you want, you can even conclude a little contract with God, like I did. Our lives are well kept in his hands. Try it.

DISTURBANCE
Prayer in Space and Time

DOMUM TUAM, DOMINE, DECET SANCTITUDO

Metten Abbey, March 1987, 7.42am

The sacred lives in the neighbourhood. And the numinous can appear mysterious. My eyesight adjusts very slowly to the darkness, and my footsteps echo on the ancient marble slabs. The only light comes from a small source at the other end of the wide room, its ceiling arching up in ribbed vaults. There, a narrow staircase leads down through a hallway into another world. I had got up early to minister in the early Mass. I am one of the few children in whose everyday life there is any sense of the holy. And not in the form of colourful Children's Bibles or funny Jesus songs, but in the form of the huge, ancient complex of buildings in our neighbourhood – a complex where there are whole floors whose contents are a mystery. Where there are corridors into which the uninitiated are not allowed. Where there are side altars holding the bones of dead martyrs and hidden chambers in which there are piles of dusty furniture from times long past, all jammed together. Where the strangely admonitory gazes of countless generations of bearded faces silently stare out at you from black and white pictures as you walk down the corridors. In the demystified postmodern age, children can see anything relevant to them on the internet by the time they're ten. But my freezing steps tread hesitantly and echo through these inner chambers, all of them too large, all of them smelling exactly the way abbeys are supposed to smell: like incense, chalk, mould and candles. '*Domum tuam, domine, decet sanctitudo*': 'holiness adorns your house' (Psalm 93:5) is written above the Abbey Church in Metten. And the Catholic thing about it is: one must also be able to see and even to smell the Holy.

THE MASTER OF CEREMONIES

It's another world in the basement: frenetic activity in the huge kitchen. The aroma of freshly baked bread and coffee. The altar servers get a bit of breakfast before they head off to school. This practice continues throughout our years in the abbey's preparatory school.

Some of my most lasting memories come from my time there – first as an altar server and later when I was performing my mandatory civil service in the abbey – this gave me a few insights into the secret world of cloistered life in all its wonder and strangeness.

Characters like Father Notker still exist. He's a bent figure with a face like an archetypical wizard. His eyes blaze out from under thick, bushy brows and then grow slowly gentler. Father Notker is the master of ceremonies. This is a function that we no longer need for our contemporary customized Sunday liturgies, which are so often cobbled together from a loose-leaf collection of pastoral ideas. It's a function that is no longer conceivable in an age of event-style church services, driven by a 'hip' praise band and dramatic visual presentations. But it is one that has taught me something important. The master of ceremonies is, as the name suggests, the artistic director for the liturgical performance. He is responsible for the selection and preparation of the vestments, for coordinating the actions of the different participants and for instructing the altar servers. In the last of these he is zealous, sometimes even rigorous, but always with an underlying attitude that flows into everything: that this absolutely is something deeply meaningful. The posture and speed an altar server serves with is significant. It's not the walking, it's the procession itself. There's a difference. It's about the right amount of incense (it should really smoke!) and the proper timing of each movement. And there are several of these: the baton carrier takes the abbot's baton of office from the abbot – at exactly the right moment! – (and, of course, only with gloves and wearing a special liturgical garment) so that he can then hand him the *mitra* – also at the right moment! – with a slight bow. The acolytes, the Bible carrier, the censer bearer – each has his role. And a holy order should govern it all. Trainers are unthinkable. Because reverence for the invisible is expressed in what is visible. And Father Notker watches everything with a strict eye, peering out from a small window in the sanctuary, in order to give 'constructive criticism', or praise, after the solemn High Mass.

I will never forget the fit of anger of this little monk, as he ran up with a crimson red face to us altar servers. Each one of us deserved a box on the ears. How sloppily we had stood around! Our folded hands had just hung limply downward instead of being raised upright, pointing to heaven. 'You're not praying to the Devil below, but to the Lord God, above!' the master of ceremonies hissed, in his nagging Lower Bavarian dialect.

And yet Father Notker is anything but hard-hearted. He just cares about the Mass. And it has to be done right. In Gregorian Chant: fitting for the current feast in the Liturgical Calendar. The unforgettable triple '*Hodie*' in the '*Magnificat*' antiphon during the vesper services on the first day of Christmas. The vestments lie ready in the chapter hall before the start of the liturgy, and each one has a little slip of paper on it that says, in red and black typewritten letters, which liturgical role it is intended for. During liturgy, the instructions are only whispered. And that in Latin, of course – '*Genuflex*'. Two decades after liturgical reform, the more prosaic term 'kneel' is still not used here.

And there's a soft heart beating in Father Notker. One day we both stay back in the choir stall after Sunday Vespers. On this occasion the monk is not wearing his simple everyday habit, but the richer black cowl that is bestowed when a monk makes his perpetual vows. When I ask him about it, Father Notker points to it and says with a gentle smile, 'This is my wedding suit.' From the mouth of this old Bavarian Benedictine who enjoys a dark beer and a hearty meal, this sentence, with all its frailty, sounds so unsuspicious and thoroughly true.

CAESURAS IN STONE

I love monasteries and have visited them all over. In Italy, decorated with ancient paintings. In France, sunk in isolation. In Germany, sobering and constant. In Greece, smelling of incense and lamp oil. In Ireland, half overgrown, and in Egypt in the blazing sunshine – the monastic traditions of these countries are linked in a mysterious way since time immemorial, pre-dating the Migration Period of the Germanic peoples – what the Romans called the 'barbarian invasions'. They are mysterious places, their stones wreathed in silence.

I love monasteries and have always found them to be a counter-cultural model, not only to a narcissistic society, but to a narcissistic church. A monastery is a baffling disturbance in the context of modern civilization. Orders of men or women who live together in celibacy and without personal property. No possessions and no descendants. Whose days are structured around prayer. Whose lives are voluntarily submitted to a collective rule, which, it is expected, will unmask their own narrowness of heart.

Maybe this is what shaped one of my first defining experiences of prayer: that it is a disturbance, a disruption. That it doesn't make any sense. And that it turns normal rules on their heads. I did not just come to understand in theory that prayer is a disturbance, but I actually saw it embodied in stone in my neighbourhood. A monastery is a constant prayer that has come to life and taken material form in space. And it testifies to what prayer is always about at its core: that our world did not make itself. That our lives don't revolve around ourselves but were created to some other end. For someone else. Every hour of prayer testifies to this calling into question of our human self-assurances.

HOW EUROPE WAS CONVERTED

The Abbey in Metten was founded in the eighth century. By then, a tight network of monasteries had already spread throughout the lands of the former Roman Empire. It was these monasteries that converted Europe. I never get over this thought. Where there were isolated Christian communities during the Roman period, where itinerant Celtic monks sowed the Gospel, it is there that the monasteries shaped the spiritual, cultural and financial face of Christian Europe for centuries.

We live in a time in which the churches seem to be running out of breath. The very things the church offers that seem to be so fascinating and appealing to the 'modern world' oscillate between the banal and what are embarrassing imitations of what the world can do better, anyway. Where, today, are the people who have been witnesses to something? People who have not just taken on ideas, but have developed a lifestyle? Whose lives reveal something of the great mystery that human life is so much more than the visible and demonstrable?

And ultimately: where are the places in which this becomes visible in time and space? Where are the spiritual vertices? Where are the places where God is worshipped simply for his own sake? Places that simply elude the earthly pattern of need and fulfilled desires?

The search for something that looks like shared spiritual life, radically lived for heaven itself, and how that can be lived out today, did not let go of me. Not from the moment my feet stepped out of that dark vaulted corridor, through the great wooden gate and into the early morning light of the abbey's inner courtyard. And it is with me today, this week, as our young staff celebrates two years of continuous prayer, and as we send off a small team to North Korea to pray in secret for the collapse of that regime. Yes, the monasteries, through their sheer existence, taught me my first lessons in prayer.

STOKING THE FIRE

Have you ever been to an abbey? If not, find out if there is one somewhere in your area and visit it. If you can, it's best to go and stay for a couple of days and not just go as a tourist. Spend some time in silence and contemplation. Even if you can only stay a short while, try to participate in choral prayer with the brothers or sisters. This is the centuries-old scarlet cord that runs through the daily life of the abbey. And if this is not possible either, then watch an online video about life in an abbey on YouTube, or perhaps the award-winning film, *Into Great Silence*.[3] The message of the abbey is one of great importance for us today.

3 *Into Great Silence*, directed by Philip Gröning, Zeitgeist Films, 2005.

GAZE
The Art of Learning to See

LEARNING TO SEE

Paris, France, June 1994

The Musée d'Orsay café doesn't breathe quite the same colonial splendour as the *Salon de Thé* in the original Mariage Frères Tea Merchants. I am a tea-lover and I have made the pilgrimage to Paris with my father. Among other reasons, I wish to enjoy something of the style of the era when Dutch sailing ships first brought Darjeeling and Oolong from the ports of India to Le Havre and Bremerhaven and here, to the most traditional tea merchant in Europe (they have 500 varieties of black and green tea!). But today we are drinking tea in the steel and glass *fin de siècle* train station that has been converted into a museum. Water lilies fill half the walls. Sensuous points of oil paint usher the eye to a surging ballroom scene. I am fifteen and enchanted by the Impressionists' hypnotic play with colour, enchanted by those alien presences that I meet in every museum, by this vast and mysterious grandeur one calls art.

Art pursues me through Paris, one way or another. It reaches out to me from a small church in the Latin Quarter with the strange, dissonant sounds of a jazz string ensemble with a postmodern edge. On the bank of the Seine and in Montmartre it is painted on the ground and on easels, in the Sainte-Chapelle translucent in the stained glass, and in the Mariage Frères Tea House, in the form of 'L'art français du thé' (as it really is written on the wall!), celebrated in a hundred varieties and carefully selected forms.

And later, when an older artist lovingly teaches me perception, seeing, structure and design in private tutoring week after week, teaching me with paper and brush, it seems like an initiation into a holy cult. A cult I can no longer escape. I walk outdoors for hours, studying the forms and colours of the leaves. I invest my pocket money in gouache, brushes and watercolours. When I'm drifting off to sleep I start to dream of pictures that I can paint. That I must paint. But more about that in a later chapter …

BURLAP, WOOD, WIRE AND PAINT

The first decisive experience happens in the Centre Pompidou, that Parisian museum for modern art that seems so confusing and bizarre from the outside. Unforgettable: *Monochrome* by Yves Klein. A picture that is completely blue. Just blue. Weird. Startling. One floor up: a class of school children standing around a sculpture. Primary-school-aged children. And the sculpture? An abstract arrangement of burlap, wood, wire and paint. A knot. Splashes of colour. Nails. What is it? And how does a teacher think he is going to get little kids interested in *that*?

From a few steps away, my father and I watch the scene with interest. The teacher begins to ask questions. But not the typical classroom questions: 'What is this trying to say to us?', or: 'What might this represent?' But instead: 'What is it made of? What materials? What colours do you see? What forms? Is the plastic rigid or flexible? Hard or soft?'

The children, at first standing around completely uninterested, now draw nearer. Their expressions become more focused. How many colours can they discover here? And what is hidden under the piece of burlap? Clay or loam? Or is it a lump of painted metal? What material is it? And how was it made? Just look at all this stuff! I am just astonished. This teacher has been able to awaken a sense of art in these children. But how? He didn't start by telling them how it was made or giving them an interpretation. He just guided them into *seeing* by using simple questions.

An introduction to art begins with learning how to see. It is not interpreting, construing and understanding that teach you the secret. The real starting point is seeing, perceiving what is really there. A work of art is its own message. It does not require our own personal interpretation to be stamped immediately on it (which puts *us* in the centre of things), but should instead be seen and appreciated for what it is.

ART

At the time, I could only imagine the depth and profoundly mystical significance of this little lesson in dealing with art. Today it seems to me to have been one of the most important steps on the path to true prayer.

God is a great artist. Everything he has created is beautiful. This is quite easy to prove: whenever and wherever you encounter something ugly, it is, most likely, something man-made. Everything in nature bears God's unmistakable signature: that of beauty.

Admittedly, man is the only creature that perceives beauty. No animal in the world stands enthralled at the majesty of the sun setting slowly over the sea. No animal collects seashells simply because they are beautiful.

Man was created with a sense of beauty by a God of beauty. And beauty wants to be seen, to be named. Calling that which is beautiful, 'beautiful', is an act of utmost truth. At the same time, it is something that brings joy and happiness. What a shame it is to enjoy a wonderful meal and not to be able to talk about it. And what a joy it is to be able to give a beautiful woman a sincere compliment.

But beauty can only be perceived if we learn to see. Indeed, the ability to perceive the beautiful as beautiful begins only when we learn to see. And learning to see means this: looking away from myself in order to look at something else. It means putting my own interpretations and ideas aside entirely for a moment and giving room to that with which my gaze presents me, here and now.

That's how art wants to be observed. 'What is this picture trying to say?' is always the wrong question. Because if the artist had wanted to 'say' something, he could have just written an academic text on the subject. And when we answer this question, a work of art far too easily becomes a canvas onto which we paint our own interpretations. Real reflection on a work of art, however, opens itself to the new, the intangible that confronts me. You only really perceive something when you receive it: when you allow it to exist as it is and accept it.

PERCEIVING BEAUTY

Prayer is talking with God. You hear that a lot. And sure, having a trusting, unguarded conversation with him as with a good friend is an important element of prayer. But talking to God can become something of a monologue. It can turn God into merely a mailbox for all of my thoughts, in which my needs and my desires are the only topics ever discussed. It can turn into me talking to myself, about myself, all the time.

Even thinking about God is a long way from actual prayer. We can see this clearly in our relationships with other people; I can think in great detail about a person standing next to me without really entering into a relationship with him. It's the same with God. Thinking about him is a far cry from having a relationship with him.

What is prayer, then?

Prayer begins with, and lives by, perception. At first, perception of what is immediately present – the beauty of nature, the air that I can breathe – but ultimately, of the sheer self-evident fact that the world exists and that I exist. This all exists, and he gives it to us. And I accept it, and I perceive it and I receive it with thanks. Anyone who perceives the world this way is just a small step from perceiving the presence of God. The God of existence gives his presence freely to those who seek him. Learning to perceive his presence is the key to a prayer that is no longer about performance or effort, but about seeing something beautiful and calling it beautiful. Thanksgiving and praise well up spontaneously out of a heart that has learned to perceive beauty.

THE IRRESISTIBLE DRAW

Paray-le-Monial, Burgundy, July 1994
Here I kneel in my hippie clothes in the chapel in which Jesus is said to have appeared to Marguerite-Marie Alacoque, back in the seventeenth century. Several times. And in such a way that was unheard of at that time. He showed her his heart. His heart that

burned fervently with love and compassion for mankind. Marguerite was stricken and carried into a flaming sea of passion.

I woke up early. Somebody had told me that there was something special about praying at three in the morning. And so here I am kneeling on the cold marble. In the light of a few candles on the altar I see the monstrance in which Jesus is adored in observation and worship.[4] I understand very little of the theory behind all this. And yet something happens inside me. I can't take my eyes off it. It's as if my eyes are drawn to this sea of fire in his heart. I can't tear them away. The endless ocean of the love of God.

It's an hour and a half before I can even stand up. And since then everything has been different. Like the eyes of a man who's gazed at the sun too long. Something stays with me and never leaves: the longing to see him.

THE 24

Croatia, August 1994
My eyes sweep over the unfathomable reaches of the gleaming sea. I am sitting on a hotel beach in Croatia and my heart is filled with longing. I write my first poems in my diary and rhyme clumsily, in German: '*Where the horizon vanishes into the grey, until I reach bliss, that's where I'll stay.*' Outwardly, my appearance is still quite colourful, (with long hair and brightly-coloured clothes – the photos are quite embarrassing for me today, and I now understand why a hotel employee came up to me one evening and suggested I participate in their beauty pageant ...) but inwardly, I am so stirred by my first experiences in prayer that I am on a painful search for more of God.

And now Croatia. In these days on the beach I read a chapter that will shape my views on God and worship forever. The first teaching I will ever give comes out of this experience. I don't understand a lot of it at the time. Even the chapter title – 'He Who Reigns' –

---

4 In the Catholic understanding Jesus is bodily present in the form of the Eucharistic host.

sounds really strange. The last sections of Romano Guardini's *The Lord*[5] deal with Jesus Christ in the depictions of his sovereignty and power in the Revelation of St. John. Not exactly light reading. But that does not bother me – I already read it with my friends in the youth centre.

But now Romano Guardini opens up something like a 3D picture for me. He Who Reigns: Revelation 4. The speech from the throne. And before him twenty-four elders, also enthroned. These aren't helpless slaves cowering in the dust before the face of God, but kings enthroned in his presence. A scene full of majesty and solemn peace. There they sit, kings before the one great King. But the natural reaction of those who sit enthroned before the One Ruler is to bow as deeply as they can, to fall prostrate. Not because they must. Yet before the overpowering majesty of the Lord, everything that would be great and magnificent anywhere else becomes insignificant. They cast their crowns down. What a wonderful statement! They are wearing crowns. Crowns which he himself has put on their heads.[6] But they lay them down, they cast them at his feet. They want him alone to be exalted and for him alone to rule.

This picture and Guardini's simple explanation have never faded from my mind. Lord, I thank you for all the dignity and the calling you crowned me with. Thank you that I have worth and greatness in your eyes. But I cast all of it at your feet. Not out of feelings of inferiority, but as a completely logical reaction to who you are and what you have done. You are God and I am not. I am mortal, and you are endless, eternal and limitless. Even vaster than the glittering sea in front of me. What foolishness and incredible obtuseness it is for us creatures to think of ourselves as the centre of our own lives. You are the real centre. The real sun in the solar system of our universe. Of course I'm going to lay down my crown.

5 Romano Guardini, *The Lord*, (Gateway Editions, Regnery Publishing, Inc, 1996).
6 Baruch 5:1-6, The Jerusalem Bible (Darton Longman & Todd Ltd, 1966).

Years later, in 2006, I wrote this praise song:

Who can praise you enough, Lord?
Bow low enough before you?
Whose hands are clean in your sight?
Heavenly majesty,
All that is great and good
Before you becomes meaningless and vain.
And I lay down my crown,
I lay down my very life,
I lay down my dreams and everything I am
At the feet of Jesus.
Worthy is the lamb.

But this is not an act of slavish abjection before an all-powerful despot against whom one does not even stand a chance. What is true greatness? What is this greatness that brings me to my knees?

Who can understand your cross?
Who emptied himself like you did?
Who can grasp what you have done?
Measureless riches and power
You set aside, you came to the earth,
As a servant, as one of the poor.

'... for your sake he became poor, so that you through his poverty might become rich' (2 Corinthians 8:9). What a grippingly simple statement of the world-shattering idea that the limitless, all-powerful God of the universe bends down into the grime of the earth to kiss his fallen creation!

'And I lay down my crown, I lay down my very life, I lay down my dreams and everything I am ...', I still sing it today and we all sing it in the Augsburg House of Prayer. And we would rather do nothing else with our entire lives than sing this: nothing other than cast our crowns, dreams, ambitions, imaginations, sense of superiority at his feet, again and again, like plastic crowns at a Mardi Gras party – that would be the greatest act of wisdom.

Everything starts, stands and falls with the art of seeing. Seeing the beauty of creation. The beauty of art. The beauty of a person. And ultimately, to see ever more clearly the beauty of the source of all of this other, created beauty. The beauty of the eternal God. And then the beauty of this one, unique person. The beauty of his words and deeds. The beauty of the man in whom God, in his fullness, became visible. Learning to see Jesus Christ. In his majesty and his humiliation on the cross. Again and again this seeing produces the only appropriate reaction from the created: praise, homage, worship – prayer.

STOKING THE FIRE

Two brief exercises can help with 'learning to see'. Take some time to look at a work of art. You can go to a museum or just look at a coffee table book about art. Take the time to fully perceive what you see there. Don't just glance at it quickly. Try not to judge it ('That's good art, that's kitsch, that's exaggerated …'), not to explain it ('This means that and that means …'), and not to classify it ('Typically baroque!'), but just accept the work of art as it is. Take your time.

A second brief exercise: read a passage from one of the four Gospels and watch Jesus. The point here is not to understand it ('What is this passage trying to say to me?') – just let the scene play out before your mind's eye. What is Jesus doing? How does he act? What does he say? You will gradually notice that learning to see has an existential quality that can immediately influence our enjoyment of life, our human relationships and our prayer lives.

AROMA
Prayer and Pleasure

COMPLEX AROMAS

Beaune, March 2003

The beauty of this place is still a bit muted this morning. Early morning fog snuggles against the terraced vineyards and dew lies on the fences. American bombs are falling in Baghdad and we are stamping through vineyards. How full of contrasts life so often seems.

On this particular day in March, I am to receive one of the most important lessons about beauty. The drive through the labyrinthine side streets of the villages is unforgettable. The vineyards begin directly behind the houses. The most expensive square metres in white wine production in the world.

Wine is an interesting thing. In the Old Testament book the Song of Songs one finds an astounding statement: 'Your love is better than wine' (Song of Songs 1:2 ESV). To my mind this is a very serious compliment. Better than *every* wine. And there are some very, very good ones, and some very, very expensive ones.

But the good, the beautiful and the worthy do not make themselves known to everyone, and not immediately. I learn this lesson in a wine cellar. In the wine cellar of one of the most famous winegrowers, in one of the most famous wine-growing cities in the world, to be precise. Beaune, the heart of the Côte d'Or, the finest wine-growing region in Burgundy.

How I got there is another story. But after visiting the vineyards of Chassagne-Montrachet and Pommard, we are now standing in a damp, half-darkened underground chamber. In front of us there are gigantic wooden casks that bear labels like 'Aloxe-Corton' or 'Musigny'. Names that quicken the pulse of every wine connoisseur.

We begin with a relatively simple Chardonnay. Our eloquent guide pours out the dregs onto the grey gravel in which the heavy casks rest. This wine is just meant to wake up our taste buds, to let them know that they should expect something. But we don't yet know what awaits us.

Endless long rows of wooden casks. Like catacombs, or like a museum, an almost sacred stillness enfolds them. It flows from a faucet into our glasses, this bright red burgundy that is so typical of the region (is it a Nuits-Saint-Georges?) with its nearly orange sheen (or is that the dim light of the cellar?). And now, definitely not too much smiling or small talk. I imitate the connoisseur with a critical gaze and reverent wafting of the aroma.

After a few seconds I reach the inescapable conclusion: it smells like wine. Definitely. The first sip confirms my assessment: the liquid tastes like wine, like red wine, even. It's not a bad wine, certainly. What an honour to be allowed to taste wine here.

My gaze settles on our guide. He's Indian, a former gourmet foods merchant dealing in cheese, living in France and speaking German. He's an attraction in himself. If he's invited out somewhere, and can tell from the label that he's being served a mediocre wine, it is his practice to turn it down with a polite, 'No, thank you', citing religious grounds. A joker. Now he's standing there getting more and more enthused from second to second. He gazes intensely into his glass. He inhales deeply. He seems to have discovered something incredible. But what?

'Ah', he says, his eyes directed steadily at the red liquid in the glass. And with his inimitable Indian-French-accented German he continues: 'That's phenomenal. I smell strawberries. Cherry! Blossom!' And immediately we try to smell it, too. Cherries? Blossom? Yeah, maybe with a bit of imagination. But he goes on. 'Let me be more precise: strawberry jam! With a touch of banana!' Ever more incredulous, we look at each other and try very hard to taste what is, apparently, to be tasted here. But our guide doesn't let up, 'Toast!', he shouts, enraptured. 'Hints of roasting aromas like in fresh coffee. It's a breakfast scene!'

A breakfast scene? Yes, we heard right. We thought that it was only about wine here … we inhale the aroma again and have another sip, striving for precision and sensitivity. And gradually we realize:

you know, maybe you really can detect a hint of toast here. 'I do smell banana, a little,' somebody else says. Our perception of wine gradually begins to change.

'How much does a bottle of this cost?' my courageous father dares to ask what everyone else is thinking. The answer comes with a gesture of the utmost nonchalance (and the reader may imagine the accent): 'If we were to bottle it now, maybe two or three hundred euros, but in a few years it will be a lot more expensive!'

We stand there speechless and try not to let our astonishment show (that is, we feign professionalism, assuming the poker face of a wine taster). And what strikes me most about this moment is that I would have been able to distinguish this wine from a three-euro supermarket wine, but probably not from a twenty-euro wine. And this, I fully recognize, is not because there are no differences between wines of these price classes, but simply because my palate is not trained to taste such nuances. My taste buds just cannot appreciate the real value that is there.

DULL TO REAL PLEASURE

With the words, 'Your love is better than than wine', the bride praises her beloved in the Song of Songs. And how often does the love and beauty of the Lord go unappreciated or even unnoticed in our glasses? What are we missing? The Holy Scripture draws a multicoloured, multilayered, multidimensional picture of a fascinating, gloriously beautiful God. In the unique figure of Jesus Christ, something shines out, something that everyone senses intuitively: that perfect humanity *does* exist; that a whole, healed natural world *does* exist. But what appreciation do we bring when we taste a precious drop of these biblical texts? What inner resources do we use to taste the nuances in Jesus' words? 'For it is not knowing much, but realizing and relishing things interiorly, that contents and satisfies the soul,'[7] said Ignatius of Loyola. And we?

---

7 St. Ignatius of Loyola, *The Spiritual Exercises of St. Ignatius of Loyola*, (P.J. Kenedy & Sons, 1914).

Surrounded by the beauty of nature, surrounded by the bounty of a life in which nearly everything that exists is an unearned gift – confronted with a God who became man and whose perfect life becomes tangible to us in the Holy Scripture and in the bread and wine of Communion – we stare into our glasses and don't realize what we are drinking.

We are like the people in the profound poem by Stefan George:

Having all and knowing all, they sigh:
'Paltry life! Oppression and hunger everywhere! Abundance is
no more!'
But I know of granaries above every house
Full of grain that flies and heaps up again – And no one takes
any …
Cellars under every courtyard where noble
Wine prevails and is poured out in the sand
– no one drinks it …
Tons of pure gold cast aside in the dust: people in rags graze it
with the hems of their garments – and not one sees it.[8]

LEARNING TO ENJOY

Yes, that seems to me to describe spiritual life. One begins with the simple insight: I can't taste it. Things that the authors of the New Testament letters or the Psalms praise in such ecstatic tones – they just leave me cold. But this is not because the material, in and of itself, is boring. Rather the boredom lies in me, like the dullness of the tongue of one untrained in wine tasting.

For every work of art and every thing of beauty, one principle is proven: it takes practice to really learn to enjoy it. And actually, that is the value of an orderly spiritual life in the deepest sense. If you are blinded by a neon light, you can't see the beauty of the starry firmament. Of course, the stars are much more beautiful. But to see

8 Stefan George, *Der Stern des Bundes*, Georg Bondi, 1921.

them, the 'lesser light' has to be turned off and the eye must adjust to the darkness. It's the same with our inner life: we are numbed by too much information, inwardly dispossessed by a regular dose of hustle and bustle and mindless routine. And we lose all zest for life itself. One senses this most acutely in the spiritual life. And when we no longer have any taste for God, then soon we will no longer have any taste for love of other people, service to others or for the beauty of nature and of art.

INNER GREATNESS

Again and again people tell me how great it is that I, and so many of the people around me, are still young and so full of energy and fire. 'The passion of youth' some call it. However, I have encountered many, many young people whose hearts are colder and closer to death than those of many adults. And I've met people who are seventy or eighty years old in whose hearts there is real treasure. I think of an old woman named Mrs Exner. As an ethnic German who grew up in Russia, she experienced most of the horrors a person could experience. Her family was deported under Stalin and endured years of forced labour; her father and brother were murdered just because they were of German extraction ... and yet her spiritual life was an effervescing spring. I listened to her for hours as a young man, when she would tell of how she woke up at four in the morning to pray for two hours before she bustled off to early Mass, in all weather. It was role models like this that taught me to lead a spiritual life while I was still a teenager. To set aside regular fasting days for myself. It became a fond habit to read ten chapters of the Bible every day. Within a few months I had read the entire Bible. For years I made it my goal to give God at least ten per cent of my day, that is, about two and a half hours.

It is both worthy and wise to lead a spiritual life that is ordered by certain structures. Structures *can* become legalistic and turn into a form of self-imposed slavery. But they don't have to. They can be a freely chosen expression of determined love. And over the months and years they expand the heart. They make the heart wide for the great beauty of God.

But let's remember: the objective here is not the slavish adherence to a set of religious rules! And even less about the kind of performance mentality that maintains that the eternal God can be impressed by human ascetics. The goal here is practice, training the spiritual sense of taste for the noble wine of the love of God. This is exactly what regular prayer and fasting can be.

HUNGRY FOR GOD

I learn this in a profound way in the year 2006 when someone tells me about his habit of fasting three days a week. This seems completely exaggerated, unbelievable, and yet it awakens a longing in me. I have already experienced, many times, the way that fasting generates hunger. Now, this is not exactly the deepest of insights. Of course you get hungry when you don't eat. But what does one hunger for? If you don't eat, you soon become aware that eating is about more than just nutrition. We comfort ourselves with food, we look for pleasure in food, we calm and reward ourselves with food. All of these are things that point to deep-seated, elemental needs in humans. Abstaining from food makes one acutely aware of all of these things. When you turn out the 'lesser light', your eyes see only darkness at first. But it is exactly this darkness that prepares your eyes for starlight. It is knowledge born of experience that can be tested over and over again: fasting makes you hungry for God and sensitive to him.

Spurred on by this knowledge, I begin to abstain from all meals except supper four days a week. I do not think that there is only one precise and correct form of fasting. Instead, I would encourage everyone to find a form of fasting that works for them. I noticed quickly that if I drink a lot of water, I can handle a whole day until around 7pm pretty well. At first I just get hungry but at the same time, I dedicate myself more intensively to prayerful meditation on the word of God.

And that, combined with fasting, awakens a new love for Jesus in me, and deepened insight, and this feeds the majority of my lectures and short teachings – something I don't want to miss. I have continued this fasting practice for many years and can tell you that my heart has learned to enjoy God more because of these times. His love is better than any expensive wine.

STOKING THE FIRE

If you would like to give new impetus to your spiritual life, make a decision, something concrete. 'If the fire is about to go out, you should put another log on', teaches Thérèse of Lisieux. By concrete, I mean a definite decision, a new step of surrender. It could be to get up a bit earlier and start a daily prayer time. For things like this it can be of great help to set a specific time and place. If there are days that are so full that no prayer time, or only a very short one, is possible, it is important to set up planned oases in the week as a whole, times in which one can come to rest and spend time with God. Basically, my experience is that short prayer times only make it harder to really 'come down'. Half an hour seems a reasonable minimum time. With a little skill and planning, this length of time should be possible for most of us, even with a busy work life and children. A fixed place is also helpful for most people: a small, nicely appointed Jesus-corner with candles and a Bible can be a visible reminder of the inner place in our heart where God is waiting for us.

A new step of surrender might also mean trying something new in Bible study, fasting and worship – something that jolts my heart out of its state of apathy. It's important to set clear, realistic goals so that this does not remain just a pious wish. In all of this it is never a case of trying to impress God with my performance; the point is to make my heart available to enjoy his beauty through collaboration with his grace.

ENIGMA OF LIGHT
Prayer in the School of the Mystics

LUNCH WITH THE MYSTICS

On the Danube near Regensburg, August 1995
I loved them from the very beginning: those 'freaks', those insane lovers of God, to whom the church posthumously assigned the amiable word 'mystic', after they had been completely misunderstood and largely dismissed as total loons by their contemporaries. The first of these friends of God that I became acquainted with were already in heaven when I met them. Nevertheless, their stories rubbed off on me, just as if I had met them while they were still alive. What John of the Cross wrote about the heart, the gentle wounding flame of love[9] – it sounded so familiar. Where he contemplated the purifying effect of grace on the soul or where he traced the inner fortresses of selfishness and pride with merciless clarity, even in the spiritual life – there I recognized, so clearly, the contours of my own inner portrait.

THE CAESURA

I will never lose the indelible impression that Carlo Carretto's *The God who Comes*[10] made on me. What the abbot said to Carlo as, after a life full of success and action, he prepared himself to begin the life of a hermit living in the Algerian desert and seeking only God, is inextinguishably imprinted on my mind. 'You have to make a break, Carlo.' Shortly after that the hot wind of the Sahara drove the ashes of the pages of his notebook into the distance. It had contained more than a thousand addresses of friends, and he quietly burned it behind a dune.

9 From the poem 'Living Flame of Love'.
10 Carlo Carretto, *The God who Comes* (Orbis Books, 1974).

I made a break too, if not such a massive one. I broke off a relationship with a nice girl, threw away some CDs and changed a few habits, all of which led to me become, increasingly, an outsider in my class.

Of course, this phase saw no lack of youthful exaggeration that I can only smile about today – as I will likely smile about the imbalances of my current phase in a few years. My offensive manner also contributed to making me appear increasingly dubious to those around me.

And yet this was a real break. I did not want to go back; I wanted more of God. This thirst for him drew me to the books of these men and women who obviously knew him better than I did. There I found perspective, an objective: one day I wanted to love Jesus just as they had.

BARBARA

This thirst also drew me to those mystics who are still living on this earth. Barbara Busowietz, a hermit living near Regensburg, is one of them. Her body, weakened by sickness, seems almost as transparent and fragile as glass. Her voice is soft but just as penetrating as her gaze. She is one of those who has been wounded by God. One whom his voice has singled out. And one who spends many hours every day in adoration and stillness, and who often cannot endure a lot of activity, not even loud worship, out of yearning for his simple presence. Mystery surrounds her. She is one of those people in whose presence even friends guard themselves against banal words and occasionally lower their gaze. Jesus has taken her deep into the fellowship of his suffering. Deep into the mysteries of love between God and the soul. Her writings are unsettling and fascinating at the same time: spiritual diaries from times of silence and prayer given in Eucharistic Adoration that last for days. Unsettling and fascinating are her descriptions of her pain, hardly bearable, when these times ended. A torturous longing. The blood red hue of love and suffering suffused with love run through all of the lines of her poetry, which I soon learned to love.

I spend several days with her in the guest room of the rectory, in which her hermitage is also located. These are the days in which I stay up to eight hours a day in silent prayer, days that shape me and wound me to this very day. And there's Irish stew for lunch. It's a unique, unforgettable scene: being with a living saint who seems to live more in heaven than on earth, sitting at the table with her, eating spoonfuls of stew … Barbara speaks with laughing eyes, constantly friendly. Something simple, girlish, hovers around her, even in her illness, and above the table is written her quote: 'Lord, make me worthy to serve your church when she is down'.

Nothing about the hermitage is narrow-minded. Everything reflects her intellectual catholicity and openness. Barbara is well-educated, and as a young woman she rejected spiritual books in spite of their good content if she found their linguistic style ineloquent. She recommends Paul Claudel to me, enraptured by his perfect style. And yet the Lord led her into a deep simplicity in which nothing unreal can remain. A total simplicity that is reflected in her books, her clothing and her hermitage. Simple and real. How she relates to the simple farm women in the village, with the scraggy dog and then with the sixteen-year-old in the wild clothes that I was: all this is no less deep and real than her prayer life, nothing in it is eccentric or withdrawn. She herself and the landlord, Father Gustav Krämer, are Catholic 'Charismatics from the very start'. They are the types who were already caught up in the Pentecostal wave that swept over the Catholic Church at the end of the 1960s – what we call 'the early years'.

Gustav's stories about the Jesus People are unforgettable – they who, in Australia, first really taught him about faith. He tells one story of a long-haired hippie who left an outdoor event to drive back into town on his huge Harley Davidson, but then came back saying: 'O Jesus, I forgot my sword!' and then grabbed his Bible.

Father Gustav loves the word of God. And he loves the presence of the Holy Spirit. He has experienced so many miracles that he can playfully fill every lunchtime with stories about them. He also loves his church. The church that has disappointed and wounded him in so many ways. With the same natural demeanour with which I see him lead the Palm Procession in the little Lower Bavarian village on Palm Sunday, he departs for Toronto in the summer of 1996. With the same natural demeanour with which he administers and gives the sacraments, he enthusiastically tells of the work of God at the 'Airport Christian Fellowship' – among Protestant Charismatics. And of the new hope that he has. And of the certainty which God has given him anew that revival will come to Germany. Sooner or later. He says this again and again. But when he does, his eyes open wider than usual when he speaks and shine more brightly. And this shine has not diminished a bit in his eyes or Barbara's, although in just a few years they will both leave this world for their true home.

As a small child, Barbara had already experienced the expulsion of Germans from East Prussia, seen her father taken prisoner and lost her home. And to his dying day, Gustav does not stop telling of Australia and the waves of revival that he experienced there. They are both true mystics of a quality such as this world does not deserve. They are home now. They have given me something that I will never lose. And yet I miss those lunches with them.

What Barbara taught me most of all was an unfathomably deep love for her bridegroom, Jesus. A love that did not let itself be shaken by her severe illness and the inner darkness that she so often experienced, but instead shone so much brighter. She was the first person to introduce me to the writings of John of the Cross. One of the main lessons that mystics teach is that there are stages in spiritual life. Phases of intense closeness to God alternate with those of the desert and the night. And there is divine wisdom in this.

The surprising and sometimes incomprehensible nature of God's leading reminds me to this day of a short adventure in a distant land. Admittedly it did not have any direct spiritual meaning, but it left a deeply significant impression.

SEASONS

Vang Vieng, Laos 2002
The air in a stalactite cave is quite different from that in the jungle. This realization should not surprise me. But I wince slightly when my

sandals slide from the last rung of the bamboo ladder to the damp floor of the cave entrance. Splash. The dry cold suddenly surrounds me, just as suddenly as the total darkness. Miles of biking and then hiking through the tropical forest, following snaky lines on a hand-drawn map. Hot, humid air. We are now in a very poor country in southern Asia, hundreds of miles from the nearest modern city. I have been married to my wife, Jutta, for a year and she has already had to get used to my penchant for adventurous trips. Her intense dislike of snakes is put to the test as we forge deeper and deeper into the humid thickets of the mountainous forest.

But the fascination of the new, the excitement of the foreign, drives me further and further into journeys like this one. Thankfully, Jutta has come along. And doesn't the journey into prayer owe something to this yearning to forge ahead into the unknown? Again and again, I have learned a lot about prayer on trips like this one. And so our route leads us deep into this impenetrable jungle with its moist heat.

Yet now it is cold and dark. The cave lamp casts a brownish circle of light on the stone walls. Otherwise it is completely dark. My steps lead me forward hesitantly. The floor of a stalactite cave is not level. It is uneven, slippery and barely visible to me. And yet I go on. Now night and complete stillness enfold me. A strange feeling comes over me: what happens if the lamp goes out? With the exception of this dull spot ahead of me, my eyes see no more than those of a blind man might. Being unable to see is disturbing. As is this cold. I can hear my heart beating. I stumble, feel my way along the damp stone wall, trying to see something. Deeper and deeper into this cave, deeper into the darkness that surrounds me like thick wool. In spite of the cold, sweat beads up on my forehead. My nervous system is tense. I bend around another crag in the cave wall, seeing only a small part of it …

Shock! Suddenly a huge white face stares at me, right in front of me. I flinch. But it is neither human nor animal … In the middle of this dark cave in the middle of the jungle there is a huge, white plaster statue. A gentle, smiling Buddha in the dingy beam of light cast by my caving lamp. I take a relieved breath, relieved and yet taken aback. Taken aback by the sudden presence of this silent colossus. Just as it had always been, there, silent, in the midst of my tapping and wandering around.

This sudden darkness – the uncontrollable, and the sudden confrontation with something wholly *other* – reminds me so clearly of experiences that are part of every life in prayer and which I had to go through for the first time years ago …

DARK AUTUMN

As suddenly as joy in prayer came, it left. I walked into the darkness unprepared and it came with a shocking abruptness. What a pleasure the first months of my new-found prayer life had been. What peace I had found, just being before God! What fascination for the Bible and talking about God! But autumn comes abruptly after summer, and the migratory birds have departed while I am thinking there is still time to swim.

I am in a new class now. Suddenly I don't have any friends. And just as suddenly there is a lot of hostility towards me, the aloof Christian. The end of a relationship. And in all of this is the sense that I am praying to a wall.

It's dark all around me and the darkness is suddenly there. I don't understand these words and yet I sense wisdom when I read the lines in which the bride in the biblical Song of Songs finds herself abandoned by her beloved in the middle of the night:

All night long on my bed
I looked for the one my heart loves;
I looked for him but did not find him.
I will get up now and go about the city,
through its streets and squares;
I will search for the one my heart loves.
So I looked for him but did not find him.
SONG OF SONGS 3:1–2

But why now? Why does this darkness come now after I just made such a radical decision for you? Why now – after this long, exhausting path through the jungle, this cave? Why, now, this darkness – when I need the light more urgently than ever?

There are no quick answers to these questions. The answer is an encounter. An encounter with God so unexpected, so sudden and so present as the face of that plaster Buddha. The masters of spiritual life know these experiences. They call them 'nights' – a sudden withdrawal of all pleasant feelings and consolations in prayer. All perceptible presence of God, all joy in prayer, in the Mass, are gone and they leave in their wake the terrifying question of why I ever even enjoyed them in the first place. But the mystics see this experience as a necessary one. It is divine pedagogy. It is a necessary step on the way to knowing God and becoming more like him.

What are the characteristics of such 'nights'? And how do they distinguish themselves from the wholly mundane experience that prayer is sometimes difficult and dry?

Real nights come when one is particularly spiritually active – often directly after a courageous decision for God. Normal feelings of tedium and dryness in prayer almost always come from our own lack of determination. A little prayer makes one satisfied with little prayer. And it takes a certain discipline to break through this torpor. But the real spiritual nights come even when we have been wholeheartedly reaching out to God and have not let up on discipline.

Spiritual indecision and tepidness – a yearning for everything, just not for God. This is not true of a person in a real 'night'. There is a painful longing for God, everything else seems an insipid imitation. Friends, television, internet, music and even nature itself – nothing can still the screaming longing for a touch from God, such as one used to experience.

In a true night one thinks that one cannot pray anymore. In particular, orally formulated prayers appear to be meaningless. The words of the songs that caused the pulse to beat a bit faster just a few weeks ago disintegrate in one's mouth like putrid rags. In contrast to this, the wish just to be before God increases. Silent endurance is the only possible prayer, regardless of how pointless it appears.

What should one do during a night?

Do what is possible. If the accustomed form of prayer is no longer accessible, look for a new one. You should not stop praying, but try to go through an open door, not slam up against one that is closed. Often a silent waiting in one's own weakness before God is the best prayer in such a situation. 'Discouragement is the greatest danger in the spiritual life,' said Teresa of Avila. Everyone who wins the victory in such a night, wins every victory. What she means is: just keep at it, even if it is hard. Often one cannot 'do' anything at all to change this condition called 'the night', and not surrendering to discouragement is already quite significant. Persevering, not losing heart, doing what is possible and not letting oneself become confused, these are the most important rules.

Seek out the help of a counsellor. This can be extremely helpful, though admittedly good spiritual directors are rare. But it is important to seek one out, especially in such a situation. Direction often helps deprive pointless trains of thought of their power and can also shore up our courage.

Hike through the cave. This is the most important lesson. Just as my feet seemed to lose their way in the trackless darkness of the Laotian cave and I simply acted on the blind faith that there was a path and continued onward, that is how one must proceed in spiritual life. At the start, the idea that one can select a spiritual path in life predominates. But gradually one realizes: I am being led. The Way is given to me as a gift and my own walk is a constant decision to commit myself to it. Ultimately every 'dark experience' in prayer teaches me that I cannot control it, that I am not the director of my life, but instead I can entrust myself to the one who is leading me when I cannot see anything.

GOLDEN HARVEST

And so I have had to experience such 'nights' repeatedly. These strange seasons of the soul that come and go. A major Christian conference in Poland. Cold and windy. And hours of waiting in the chapel without even the slightest sense that a response was forthcoming. I stand perplexed in the middle of this celebrating crowd and ask myself what I am doing wrong because my heart is dark and cold.

But then comes the harvest. Only a few weeks later. The forest is a sea of gold, orange and red leaves around the house of the community that is hosting us. Vienna in October. Mild, sunny days. I sit in the chapel and the climate changes. The change comes suddenly. And once again this suddenness is disturbing. Deep peace. This peace that is known only to those who encounter God. The peace that destroys once and for all time the illusion that this could just be something human, something psychological. This unbelievable joy. Not joy on account of something, but joy found in everything. Everything. God is there and the minutes turn to gold. With a clarity, a depth, that I have not experienced for years. It's autumn again. But it is a wholly different season in God's calendar – it feels like spring.

What did I do to get it? Nothing. I just waited. It could have happened any day, in any simple, dry prayer time. As unexpectedly as a white face in the dim beam of light from my caving lamp in the middle of the jungle.

But it actually happens on that October day in Vienna. This day is followed immediately by a few years of the clearly perceptible presence of God. What can one learn from this? Simple: there are things that one can do and things one cannot do. We can and should develop discipline in the spiritual life. We can and should learn to pray. But God's perceptible presence remains distant from us. It's not that God adapts to our rhythm, but that we gradually adapt to his. And that is not the least of reasons why prayer is such an adventurous journey.

STOKING THE FIRE

There are different phases in spiritual life. Have you already noticed that it is not just our personal life in general, but also our relationship with God that goes through more intense and more superficial, easier and more difficult times? Merely directing one's attention to this fact can be enlightening. Why don't you pick up a sheet of paper and draw something like your spiritual path through life on it? What was the starting point? What were the decisive milestones? If you want you can use particular colours to indicate the intensity of your relationship with God or your perceived closeness to God. Have you experienced such phases of apparent distance from God in the past?

HERE AND NOW
Prayer as Contemplation

I AM

Jerusalem, July 1998

The wind rises in the late afternoon every day. It smells of cedar and acacia. In the late afternoon I always sit on the roof terrace and drink tea. The day has been oppressively hot. One of my jobs as a volunteer in the Benedictine Abbey is cleaning. And there is dust and sand everywhere, blown in by the wind of the Judean Desert. In thick, ochre-coloured borders, it deposits itself along the windows and in the corners of the rooms. And I spend hours sweeping it away. It turns the wash water in my bucket brown, only to return a few days later as a film on the freshly cleaned glass.

In the hot afternoons I wander through the old city of Jerusalem, with its walls and ruins. And somehow, I feel like one of these stones dozing in the heat. For weeks I have been staying in this abbey waiting for an encounter with God, and I am still waiting. Every morning I get up early and participate in the Mass. Afterwards I pray the hours, work, pray some more, read the Bible and walk the streets that Jesus walked. But he is not there in person: 'You are looking for Jesus the Nazarene, ... He is not here' (Mark 16:6). So I sit on the roof terrace and enjoy the wind as it finally cools down and sip the dark brown Assam in my cup.

'*My walls are silent in the dusty light. I wait for you. I have waited for your face for thousands of years ...*', I write a line of poetry in my diary and find myself identifying with this city in which God's presence was found so often, missed so often, and squandered so often.

Every evening I then spend an hour in the small chapel and kneel on the warm stone floor. The faint aroma of rose incense and pine, the alternating tones of car horns, church bells and the call of the muezzin – just Jerusalem. I kneel here like this, every day. Here I kneel for about an hour and I don't know what I should do. The same old question, the details are just hammered out differently, again and again: what is prayer? And how does it work?

Apart from me, there is no one in the chapel. Only the abbot, a man still relatively young, whose tall form, clad in his grey habit, radiates dignified peace. He kneels beside me on the floor every day and seems to be praying. At one point he turns to me and asks very softly:

'Johannes, what do you do when you pray?'

The question overwhelms me with its non-threatening force. Yeah, what is it I am doing, actually? When my answer turns out to be a bit woolly, he offers to meet with me daily and give me instruction in prayer. I am perplexed and desperately need a new touch from God, which is why I accept thankfully, like a thirsty man accepting a drink of water.

My first hour of prayer under his direction is the very next day. It goes quite differently from how I expected. The first thing is that Abbot Benedict gently points out how I am sitting – namely hunched over and on the bare floor. After this I am ready to familiarize myself with the form of prayer that I will use for the next few decades! It is important to kneel completely upright and on a carpet. So my first hour of prayer consists of kneeling upright, arrow-straight on my kneeler. What an odd school of prayer!

It is even stranger the next day. God is in the here and now. And he dwells in my inner being, in my body, the temple of the Holy Spirit. When one is wholly present in the here and now, one is open to the presence of God. So far, so good. As an exercise in getting past my constantly rambling thoughts and really coming into the present, my teacher suggests that first I really perceive what is here, now. There is a difference between perception and thought. While thoughts can ramble anywhere, perception brings one back to the present and thus back into the encounter. God is the 'I am here'. He is in the here and now. Only we, unfortunately, are usually not there. We are lost in our thoughts, which constantly carry us away to somewhere else. The simple perception of what is happening right now brings us back to the truth. The truth in which God dwells.

ITCHING

All of this makes sense. Yet the coming days prove strenuous. I sit in the chapel one more time and try to do what the abbot told me: simply sit quietly and perceive my body. Starting at my feet, rising up through the spine to my hands and then my pulse and breathing. That is the first step. But one that does not feel at all like prayer to me. Every time I want to sit still I suddenly feel an itch somewhere. Or the sudden need to move. Don't I want to encounter God? Praise him, love him, think about him? Instead I am supposed to 'listen to the inner self', to what I can perceive about my body. And to be honest, it just seems like learning meditation to me. But is that prayer? Am I now finally falling for some esoteric, diluted form of Far Eastern religion? The only thing that keeps me there is the personality of the abbot. Love for Christ exudes from his every pore and there is something compelling about his inner peace.

My concept of prayer still has something very cerebral about it. I mean, prayer is supposed to be thinking about God. Even the idea that, in relationships between humans, there is a very marked difference between 'thinking about someone' and 'having a relationship with someone' is something I could have learned from Martin Buber. His book, *I and Thou*,[11] had shaped my thinking over the previous months. But, that the 'being there' of God is actualized precisely through my 'being here' in my body – this only becomes clear to me after the initial experience. That Paul really calls our bodies (and not reason, conscience, etc.!) the place where God dwells (1 Corinthians 6:19). And that Jesus maybe meant it quite literally when he said 'rivers of living water will flow' from his body (which is exactly what John 7:38 says) – I recognize all that only after the fact as a 'theological explanation' for what I experienced.

The actual experience is just about as ordinary as it is possible to be.

11 Martin Buber, *I and Thou* (Scribner Book Company, 1958).

IN THE AROMAS OF JERUSALEM IN THE EVENING

It is the second week of my daily exercises. They have, until now, tended to be more tedious than not. At best it has been like dutifully completing a school assignment. On this evening I kneel down one more time in the chapel. One more time, in the sounds and smells of evening in Jerusalem. As the sun gradually descends, the light of the burning oil lamp slowly replaces the deep yellow shaft of light that falls horizontally through the small window, until the dark grey of evening slowly washes out all the colour inside.

And today I try again to listen within. To that which is. To the perceptions of my own body that reach my brain. To reality. An uncomfortable preliminary exercise, but one which, to my mind, might just lead to actually learning prayer. But something else happens. My concentrated attention climbs through my feet, legs, lap and then my respiratory pathway with all of its stations. After about forty-five minutes I've perceived all of the areas of my body. Or more accurately: I let them get through to me, I only listen attentively. At the end of this time, there is suddenly a quiet certainty in the room: I am wholly here. Without anything great and extraordinary, and yet accompanied by deep peace. Simply being. And at the same time there is an even more massive certainty: God is here. His beauty, the peace of his presence, is here and it enfolds me on all sides. As is true whenever one is in God's presence, time seems to stand still and the eternal circling and running seems to condense into a single point: the here and now in the presence of God.

HERE AND NOW

This small event permanently changed my understanding of prayer. Prayer is more being than doing. And more perceiving than thinking. Prayer is not 'thinking about God', and it does not mean 'flying away to another place' inwardly. It has nothing to do with daydreaming or wishful thinking. But it has a lot to do with love.

Were I to sit in front of you for an hour and you were to speak, but I were to then remain lost in my thoughts – no encounter would take place. But if instead I was open and available for you, if I was wholly in the here and now in front of you, just giving you space, then a real relationship would develop.

It's not unusual for us to pray: 'Come close, Lord, be near to me …', and to have the impression that he is far away. But he is not far away. He is here. For the Christian, your body is the temple of the Holy Spirit (1 Corinthians 6:19). He dwells there. God is there. In the here and now. Our only problem, as I said before, is that we usually aren't.

What then is prayer? A movement of the heart that starts with coming back to what is already waiting for me. To the One who is waiting for me in the here and now. I come back to him from all the places where I have got lost. From daydreaming, worry, the expectations of others and every other form of 'chasing after the wind' (Ecclesiastes 1:17) that we call 'everyday life'.

STOKING THE FIRE

There are good books on the subject of contemplative prayer. For that reason, I will only give a word of encouragement: begin your prayer time, not by saying something to God or thinking about him, but instead just by taking time to perceive what is there. God is not in 'the great beyond', so that you first have to free yourself from everything that is here and now. He is the one who is wholly present. A return to that which awaits me in the here and now can begin with the perception of one's own body. It is always in the here and now, even if my thoughts are usually somewhere else.

Take a moment and kneel upright, for example on a kneeler. Then begin, step by step, to consciously perceive the various areas of your body. Listen to your own body: what can you feel in your feet, your neck, your hands? Proceed slowly and with keen attention. Finally, your breath: God put the breath of life in you. Follow the course of air you inhale from your nose deep into your chest.

These very simple exercises in awareness can help you to enter into the here and now consciously. This is not prayer, of course. But it is an essential prerequisite. From the position of being fully present, you can continue in prayer in practically any direction. Free, spoken prayer. Sung praise. Liturgical prayer like 'The Hours', for example. Intercession or prayer with the word of God: all of these forms of prayer become richer when you take the time to actually be fully present in the here and now. And sometimes you may even have the urge not to do much at all, but only to remain and rest in the silent presence of Jesus.

EPIGNOSIS
Prayer and Revelation

A DATE IN THE MIDDLE OF NOWHERE

Somewhere in the Syrian Desert, Autumn 1999
It grew cool surprisingly fast. Even though my light, white cotton clothing had begun to stick to me uncomfortably in the constant heat of the afternoon, I am now almost shivering – here, at the end of the world. One never forgets certain moments of prayer. For example, this one, as night falls over the desert. It's been a stressful day. A bus ride that lasted for hours. A breakdown. Waiting on the roadside surrounded by white sand and boulders. Now, it's late. An old SUV rumbles by; next to me the water pipes of the old men's shishas bubble merrily. The scent of cardamom, the sweet aroma of shisha smoke and gasoline. Life is turning out the lights and I am sitting, in the middle of nowhere, under an awning that, with a bit of imagination, one could call a café.

To encounter God, it can't be done. To hear God's voice is a gift, given to someone. So I sit here with the only book I brought with me on this trip, the New Testament, open before me. I am tired after this long day and the long journey, the noisy bus station in Damascus and the dusty heat. And yet, this evening I experience what it means for God to speak to me through his word.

My eyes glide across the page. The stars come out and yet it is not light, there where I sit.

'After this, Jesus travelled about from one town and village to another …' (Luke 8:1). As if my feet had suddenly fallen down a hole while trudging through undergrowth, my eyes come to a sudden halt. And my whole attention focuses on this sentence, which then turns into a door opening inwards. What is it about this sentence that stops me in my tracks? I sit here, tired, in the middle of nowhere in a fog of shisha smoke and read about Jesus. I read about the God who became a man who walked. About the God who became a man who travelled on foot along dusty roads between insignificant hamlets in the Near East to get to the next tiny village. To a place where five, maybe nine families were living. Unwashed children and goats on the road. Men busy farming and women breastfeeding their babies, all of them uneducated. I sit in a café in an insignificant little town in the Syrian desert and read about a God who became man, to walk around insignificant hamlets. Because a few people lived there. And 'from one town and village to another'; it was not something he did only once. It was not the first-century equivalent of a PR visit by some celebrity to some disaster area. It was just one more day. One more arduous foot march. Like every morning.

What happens to me while I sit there? I don't understand it. But suddenly this God-become-man is so near to me. Jesus, who are you that you hike on foot between dusty, insignificant little villages to speak with just a handful of people? You, through whom everything was created ... You, before whom every knee will bow ... You, within whom, I read, the fullness of divinity dwells?

And while the muezzin, in a crackling recording playing far too loud over loudspeakers, tells of a God who knows nothing of being human, I encounter precisely this God-become-man, as if he were an old acquaintance who sits himself down with you at a stranger's table out in the Syrian desert. How do I encounter him? I don't know. But suddenly I understand more, no, I suddenly *feel* more of what love means. But it is no abstract understanding. I feel like someone who just met with someone. And while tears come to my eyes, I repeat: "'After that Jesus wandered from one town and village to another ...'" The next morning Jesus continued onward ... You went onward ... You continued onward ... Jesus, you went far enough to find insignificant people whom you wanted to encounter ... Jesus, you went far enough to find me ... to find me here in the middle of nowhere.'

(EPI)GNOSIS?

That evening I learned to distinguish between knowing and comprehending. I had already read this Bible passage many times, I knew it. And yet on that evening in the desert something changed. I will never read this passage with the same eyes as before. I have learned to distinguish between head knowledge and heart knowledge. And I have learned that I have too much of the former and far, far too little of the latter.

The language of the New Testament has two terms that are translated as 'knowledge' in our English texts: *gnosis* and *epignosis.* And yet the two terms do not mean exactly the same thing. *Gnosis* means a certain intellectual insight or realization. It can be positive, but it can also lead to arrogance (1 Corinthians 8:1). Paul also uses the word *epignosis*, which is the word *gnosis* amplified with the prefix *epi*, which just means 'above' or 'about'. Paul always uses this word in a positive sense and when it is used, it means more than intellectual realization: it appears in these cases to refer to revelation!

What does 'revelation' mean? It means that there is a God who reveals something about himself. In the case of purely intellectual knowledge, the deciding factor is the mind of the person who knows. In the case of *epignosis*, though, the deciding factor is that God reveals something. The following Bible passage deals with *epignosis* and it revolutionized my understanding of reading the Bible:

> *For this reason, ever since I heard about your faith in the Lord Jesus and your love for all God's people, I have not stopped giving thanks for you, remembering you in my prayers. I keep asking that the God of our Lord Jesus Christ, the glorious Father, may give you the Spirit of wisdom and revelation, so that you may know him better.*
> EPHESIANS 1:15–17

The word that Paul uses in this passage is *epignosis*.

What characterizes this type of knowledge?

At first this is knowledge of 'himself' – this means that one has knowledge of God himself and not just interesting facts. I find it astonishing that such knowledge is apparently within the capacity of the human mind.

This knowledge is imparted by the 'Spirit of wisdom and revelation' – it is a knowledge that the Holy Spirit imparts, not human intellect alone.

Paul prays for this knowledge. Clearly it is not something that can simply be conveyed in words. Otherwise he would have written: 'Therefore, I would like to impart to you knowledge of God, for which reason I will now explain everything important about the subject.' Paul believes that one can only ask God for this kind of knowledge.

He continues:

I pray that the eyes of your heart may be enlightened in order that you may know the hope to which he has called you, the riches of his glorious inheritance in his holy people, and his incomparably great power for us who believe. That power is the same as the mighty strength he exerted when he raised Christ from the dead and seated him at his right hand in the heavenly realms, far above all rule and authority, power and dominion, and every name that is invoked, not only in the present age but also in the one to come.
EPHESIANS 1:18–21

Wow, these words are positively vertigo-inducing! Somehow this all sounds very complicated and very grand. But do they not awaken a longing in us? To have our eyes enlightened? To know the immense glory of our inheritance in Jesus? The greatness of his power? The immeasurable hope that is in him?

I think that God would like us to find an approach to the Bible that would make much of what Paul is praying for here real to us. God wants to enlighten our hearts; he wants to show us great things. I believe that God would like to speak to us through his word regularly and quite personally, just as he did that first time to me in the desert.

The difference between biblical head knowledge and real revelation (which I will refer to from now on as *epignosis*) is enormous. *Epignosis* changes something in me: it takes hold of my mental categories and makes the matter in hand become important. Head knowledge alone is dead, although it is not, in and of itself, bad: it is good to know what is in the Bible and what our creed proclaims. But that is only the beginning. Our problem is that we know everything theoretically and put almost nothing into action. Every Christian knows that Jesus died on the cross for him or her. And nearly every Christian also knows, theoretically, that Jesus' blood justifies him before God. But to what extent does this knowledge actually shape our deeds? In spite of this knowledge our lives are mostly determined by the fact that we feel great when we do something right and feel bad when we do something wrong. Deep in our inner being there is a voice that says: 'God only likes you if you constantly live the good, Christian life.' And if we fail to live up to our own high ideals, we suspect, deep in our hearts, that God is disappointed with us.

Isn't that astonishing? We know that Jesus died for us and that we do not have to make ourselves acceptable to God through our own righteousness. And yet there is clearly another theology at work in our hearts. If we really understood that Jesus died on the cross for us and God loves us unconditionally, wouldn't our lives, wouldn't our emotional worlds look completely different? We Christians in the Western world have, for too long, mistaken head knowledge for real knowledge. We think we know everything just because we have heard something a couple of times. But we know only very little.

It is one thing to know what Africa is. And quite another to have been there once, perhaps even lived there for years. We all know the message of Jesus Christ. But do we know it like a country we've only read about or have we actually been there? The confusing thing is that whether you've ever been to Africa or not is not demonstrated by the statements you can make about Africa. 'Africa is a continent', and 'Elephants live in Africa' are both true statements regardless of whether one really knows what one's talking about or not. We have learned to formulate religious sentences of this kind. Sentences that are repeated in sermons and sung in songs. And sentences that do not change our lives and don't touch our hearts at all. Head knowledge.

HIS VERY OWN KISS

How would I deal with the following situation? My wife goes to an acquaintance of ours and asks him to tell me that she'd like to kiss me. 'Well that's nice,' I would probably respond, 'but why can't she just tell me herself?'

'Which of you believes that Jesus loves you?', I once asked a group of young people at a Christian event. The majority of the young people raised their hands. The question was for me as much as for them when I responded by asking: 'How do you know that? Where did you read it? Did he himself say it to you? If not, don't be satisfied without it!'

Over the years I have been blessed again and again with experiences like the one I had in the desert: God enlightens my eyes with a specific Bible passage, he allows me to suddenly realize something in it that I had not realized the previous fifty times. I have been able to trace the following characteristics of true biblical *epignosis* in the process:

Biblical *epignosis* is non-transferable. Just as the foolish virgins (Matthew 25) in the parable have to purchase oil for their lamps themselves and can't borrow it from their companions, one can only make the journey into one's own *epignosis*. I experience it again and again. An acquaintance enthusiastically explains to me over the phone the new discovery he just made in the Bible: 'Do you understand? I no longer live, but Christ lives in me!', says the voice on the other end of the line, quoting Galatians 2:20. Sure, I know this passage myself, but the enthusiasm cannot reach me yet. Because that's *his epignosis* – I have to have my own!

Biblical *epignosis* is contagious. Nothing is as contagious as a person who has encountered God. There is a mysterious sensory organ in a human being. And this sensory organ can detect whether one is reporting something authentic or something one has just read. I've had the experience repeatedly: listeners, and especially young people, have an excellent sense for telling whether a leader, a preacher or a parent really lives and really believes what he or she says, or not. One of the reasons that so many people have stopped going to church is that they sense that there is a lot of head knowledge in the preaching but little real heart knowledge. The opposite is the case when someone tells what has been illuminated in his life. His eyes begin to shine and the listener can sense that this is more than a couple of good ideas he wrote down.

Biblical *epignosis* cannot be forced. A personal experience with the Bible cannot be produced at will. And yet there are things that put me in a position in which I am open to God's kisses. The most essential factors are:

Time: Only in the very rarest of cases does God meet me immediately, in the first few minutes that I spend in his word. It takes a certain amount of time (usually about ten minutes) to unplug and get into God's word.

Fasting: The Bible shows fasting and prayer to be basic disciplines of the spiritual life. The point of a lifestyle characterized by fasting and prayer is not to prove to God just how serious I am, but that it changes my heart and makes me ready to receive his kisses. I cannot say exactly why it is, but when you fast, you gradually sense more and more hunger for the word of God. And God loves to satisfy us with his kisses.

Prayer: The Scriptures are not meant just to convey information about God to us. Rather, the entirety of salvation history is an invitation to a relationship. In practical terms, this means that you understand more of Scripture when you start to speak with the One who inspired it. For that reason, one should not think of reading the Bible and talking with God as entirely separate, but think of them as connected.

STOKING THE FIRE

Many, many people never know the pleasure of encountering God in his word, simply because they do not know where and how to start. For that reason, I present a very simple method, that consists of two daily steps:

1. Bible reading. Begin with the Gospel of Matthew, and decide on a number of chapters to read every day. Maybe two. You can read them quite quickly or very slowly. But read!

2. Whenever you come to a passage that tells you something about God, one that invites you to believe something or even challenges you to do something, take a break. Stop and talk with God about this passage. If it is a statement about God, then thank him for this truth. Do this quietly for a minute or two. Then ask him to deepen this truth in you – for a minute or two. And if it is a statement that challenges you to do something, then decide before God to do it and ask him to help you – for a minute or two.

You will notice how this simple method helps you to write the word of God in your heart. You will not believe how much more happens, compared to when you just consume biblical information. It's also very helpful if you write down your ideas and prayers in a notebook or diary. Writing things down focuses your thoughts and helps fight distraction. You will be pleasantly surprised when you review what has happened in your heart after you've done this for three months. You will be on the way to your own *epignosis*. In the middle of nowhere, or in your own home.

THE EXPLOSION
Prayer and Power

POWER

Atlanta, January 2013

Cool metal in my hand. The smooth wood of the butt. The recoil of the M1921 Thompson submachine gun is a powerful experience the first time you fire one. Adrenaline in my veins and a certain fascinated terror at this concentrated power, fire spewing out of the barrel as soon as my finger squeezes the trigger. After so many stories of mysticism I can risk starting this chapter with a martial experience. Although it is the dream of many little boys (and certainly one of mine!), it might seem a bit strange to want to go shooting with automatic weapons. To Europeans, I mean. But in America everything is different, and I am in Atlanta, Georgia. It's just a natural part of the authentic experience of the 'American Way of Life'. Just like the steakhouse, omnipresent fast food, the expanse of the land and the ease with which everything seems to happen in the Southern States.

They look like very large boys, the heavyset dads with their baseball caps who come here on Saturdays to try out their firearms. Pithy Republican slogans adorn their overlarge SUVs, parked in front of the little store in the suburbs. Country music plays from the speakers and, with a gesture of complete nonchalance, the young salesman hands us the weapons and the eighty rounds of ammunition over the counter. Yup, we're shooting the aforementioned historical machine gun, then an *Uzi* and two assault rifles. No, this will not be followed by a treatise on gun laws and no justification of the masculine fascination with weapons. Rather a reflection on the sheer alarm that one feels when one discovers that the trigger to a tremendous power has been placed in one's hand. That's what it's about. We walk to the shooting range through narrow halls, and, after a few clumsy movements, the tommy gun is loaded and unlocked. Excitement.

You don't forget the explosive force of such a weapon. The jerk when you pull the trigger. And a millisecond later, the sudden recoil against your chest, the deafening staccato, the rattle of the casings falling to the ground in the shooting stand. The minuscule movement that sets it all in motion – and the massive effect. Terrifying and destructive as far as weapons go. And yet it compares (perhaps somewhat coarsely) to an image that comes to mind whenever I think of the summer of 1999, when I first felt the power of a different weapon. Not one that is destructive or brutal. But one whose sudden explosive power shocked and overwhelmed me just as much: the power of fasting and prayer. Don't read any further if you are easily frightened …

LONGING FOR MORE

Conspiratorial glances between my friends and me, again. Years ago. My mystical lunches and experiences in the abbey really should have been enough to turn me into a monk or a hermit. In fact, for a few years, when I was younger, I often dreamed of it; I even planned to remain unmarried, celibate. But it wasn't just the startlingly beautiful young woman I fell in love with in 1997 (and where of all places? Why, Bethany, Israel) that put the kibosh on my plans to be a hermit. Life's like that.

God, who hits straight with a crooked stick, arranged it so that the first Christian youth group that I joined after my conversion experience fell apart. And in a very ugly way. But before that, they had already thrown me out. There had been incidents that one would characterize today as 'spiritual abuse' – in any case I was considered hyperactive, pushy and overzealous. And maybe I was. And so there I was, seventeen, full of passion, full of ideas, but without a group. A while later, a few of the former members of the aforementioned youth group – Django, Ursula, Franz-Josef and myself – met coincidentally a couple of times, and we discussed how it could be continued. Over coffee we decided to meet more often. For an entire weekend. And so, spontaneously and entirely unintentionally on my part, a youth group arose under my leadership that gave itself the provocative German name 'FCKW' (which stands for *Fröhlich, Charismatisch, Katholisch sind Wir*, which translates as 'We're happy, charismatic Catholics'. We never stopped being ashamed of this name and it is still in use even today). We met at weekends, had a good time together and held worship. And from the beginning there were 'new guys' involved, other people who were friends of ours but still far from the faith. Many of them converted and everything was a great adventure. Our events grew, we had a lot of fun together and everything happened as if by itself, through teenagers – which is the dream of many youth workers. But at some point in early 1999, a couple of friends and I were sitting around at my house by candlelight. And exchanging conspiratorial glances. The beginning of a little, slightly crazy idea. I love it to this day, this Brotherhood of the Highly Dissatisfied. And brother, were we ever dissatisfied!

I had read some wild stuff. Yonggi Cho's book, *Prayer: Key to Revival*[12] with his reports of the Prayer Mountains in Korea, and about heroes of the faith like John Hyde and Daniel Nash who had all experienced God's overwhelming acts of power as a fruit of prayer. Our youth group was running well, but there was quite obviously so much more! We were dissatisfied with our own spiritual lives. We confessed to each other, quite spontaneously, what they were really like and what urgently needed to change. Suddenly there was a new enthusiasm in the room: something had to happen! But what?

I recalled all the stories I had read. In all of them persistent prayer, and in most cases fasting too, played a role. Should we try something different for once? With an adventurous gleam in our eyes we agreed: we would go on retreat together for a weekend and just fast and pray.

A thing is said, a thing is done. The result was less than impressive. The house where we stayed was poorly heated. If you're fasting, you get cold really easily. This resulted in us spending most of our day in

---

12 Paul Yonggi Cho, *Prayer: Key to Revival* (W Pub Group, 1984).

the only warm room in the building, the common room, which we had set up as a 'Prayer Room'. And so we actually prayed the whole weekend with nine people. It felt anything but special.

Nevertheless, this first minor experiment in sustained prayer changed something in us. We sensed a desire to do something like it again. And so it happened, and again this time nothing especially perceptible happened. Ostensibly, everything was just as insignificant as a finger squeezing a trigger.

HOLY CHAOS

Otzing, June 1999
In June, the next regular youth weekend is scheduled. Around thirty-five teenagers show up. Ten, for sure, are there for the first time. They trot up the stairs, lay their sleeping bags on the beds and goof around until late in the night. The meal consists of spaghetti in cream sauce with ham, and in short spiritual inputs, other teenagers tell them about God. Like every other time. And then Saturday evening comes. And with it the shock. The explosion.

The schedule for such an evening at the FCKW is rather simple: very long worship, at least two hours. That is, a guitar, Christian rock music and a lot of enthusiasm. And then the chance to make a personal decision for Jesus and receive a prayer of blessing. I am the worship leader and have written all of my songs and the planned schedule down on a piece of paper. But suddenly something very, very different happens.

Quite often we pray or sing things like 'Come, Lord!' or 'Rule among us, break in ...' – and these are all fine prayers. But I had to learn that it is quite a different thing when God *actually does it for real* ... it feels like accidentally pulling the trigger on a machine gun.

So here I stand with my guitar, surrounded by a bunch of singing young people. And if I had not been there myself, I probably wouldn't believe it, but during the second song, *HE* comes. *HE* comes into the room. And *HE* takes control. And it looks like this: without anyone touching them, people start falling over. BOOM! No, no one faints, no one loses consciousness. And nobody is pushed. The persons affected report that they were overwhelmed by God's power. It happens without any warning and, of course, without any prior agreement: all over the room young people are falling down and staying there.

Now, it's a bit difficult to run an evening effectively when all of the participants suddenly start falling to the floor. I am seized by a certain astonishment. It doesn't get any better because ... *everybody* hits the floor. Even participants who are there for the very first time and have no idea that there even is such a thing (the charismatic scene calls it 'resting in the Spirit'); none of us have experienced it in this way before. And what happened then? Well, at first a holy chaos breaks out. And I am in the middle of it, playing my guitar ...

Some just lay very quietly on the floor, and later report that they experienced the peace and love of God in a deep way. Others begin to weep loudly because God touches areas of profound pain in their souls. Others laugh because they feel God's joy in them, others have visions of spiritual reality, some for a long time. The evening goes on until midnight and just one thing becomes clear to me: someone took the leadership out of my hands! In everything, though, there is the overwhelming presence of something holy. Of some*one* holy.

After this FCKW is never the same. We experience such demonstrations of God's power at every meeting now. Young people are healed, in some cases entanglements and demonic chains are broken, prophetic impressions, visions and images are totally normal. Now, one might think that teenagers would be totally overloaded by such experiences, but we experienced the opposite. Even those who were there for the first time were not only not scared off, but were instead absolutely fascinated. In fact, the size of our group doubled in the months that followed. Very quickly I became the leader of nearly a hundred young people. I had at the time no training or education in this field at all, and I felt quite overwhelmed. I even began to pray that this intense outpouring of the Holy Spirit might stop because, as a leader, I had no idea how to deal with it. But I have learned one thing once and for all: fasting and prayer unleash a power that is totally unbelievable. You can compare it with that of a loaded firearm. The recoil is huge. I still haven't learned to deal with it well. But the yearning grew to have a place where this spiritual power could be constantly cultivated …

THE POWER OF FASTING AND PRAYER

Talking about the 'effectiveness' of prayer seems strange to many. Yes, isn't the point of prayer to get away from the idea that efficiency and productivity are supposed to govern everything we do? Actually, that's true. And many chapters of this book are dedicated to the value of that prayer whose beauty really shines when it 'has no visible objective' but is a freely given expression of love.

Sure, God is not a vending machine. Sure, it's naïve to expect an immediate miracle in response to every prayer. You hear and read this a lot. And yet we cannot escape those passages in the Bible in which God quite explicitly challenges us to ask that we might receive! The Bible even holds promises of blessing for entire nations if they repent and seek God in prayer (2 Chronicles 7:14). And this kind of prayer is associated with fasting again and again in the biblical texts (Joel 2:15). God very explicitly challenges us to ask things of him (Jeremiah 33:3), and both Jesus (John 16:24) and the Apostles (Ephesians 6:18) constantly encourage us to do this. Indeed, in the book of James, he even says that we receive nothing because we ask for nothing (James 4:2). You need to let this word really sink in: there are obviously things that God wants to give us that we do not receive because we do not ask for them. Now of course, God is omnipotent. He could just give everything to us. But something significant seems to happen when we ask for something specific. Apparently it is important to God that it be important to us, too. He longs for cooperation with us. His plans for the world are built on our agreement with his intentions. And this is exactly what intercession is about. God wants to rescue and set free – but does he find intercessors who will agree with him?

At first glance, intercessory prayer seems to be something utterly weak. Sitting down in a room and telling God what he should do –

pretty please – sounds like the exact opposite of 'effective'. And it is really scandalous to the wisdom of this world that God builds his kingdom through the weak prayers of weak people. It seems like complete foolishness that the omnipotent God acts because mortal men just ask him to. But this is exactly what the entirety of Scripture teaches. We can't escape these passages. And we can't escape the heroes of the faith throughout history who experienced exactly this. They experienced a fruitfulness and authority in their ministry that eclipses everything that most of us experience in our groups and churches.

I have already seen with my own eyes just a fraction of this. But this fraction has convinced me that the power of prayer is like the force of a fully automatic weapon. Even if prayer itself seems as insignificant as the twitch of a finger on a trigger.

STOKING THE FIRE

Have you ever consistently prayed with someone else? Just praying is worthwhile. But although I can't exactly explain why, there is a special power in persistent prayer with a group.

A suggestion: find a couple of like-minded people and hold a day of prayer, a night of prayer, a weekend or a 24/7 week in which prayer never stops! The form is of secondary importance. Either one person can take an hour for himself or several intercessors can pray together (both have advantages and disadvantages). But try something 'radical' together. Perhaps even combine it with fasting. You will see: it can be a real challenge, but it will give you a sense of the immense power that is released when weak human words agree with the intentions of God. When we pray 'Your kingdom come, your will be done', a bit more of his kingdom and will become visible. And sometimes with real power.

BREAK OUT OF THE NORMAL

Prayer and the Adventure of the New

MANY LITTLE ADVENTURES

My personal prayer story is inseparably linked with the story of the Augsburg House of Prayer. It has already been touched on at various points in this book and this chapter will recount the very beginning. The question of why people like my wife and I came to believe that young people can be called, even today, to make prayer their primary vocation, is perhaps not the most urgent to many people. Ultimately, the real question – running through all these stories – is about the true value of prayer. How far can one go and, sometimes, *must* one go, in order to put prayer at the centre? It's also about how God makes such a path to him possible and in what way he calls people to prayer today. Our little adventure with the founding of the House of Prayer in Augsburg is about all of this.

JOY, AFRICAN STYLE

Katikamu, Uganda, 5.57am, August 2003
Much too loud. And what's worse: much too early! Dazed, I roll out from under the mosquito net. It was a quiet night, really. At least we had been able to sleep more easily than the nights before. Once again, I had been a bit too optimistic in assessing the situation while we were travelling. We had driven north for hours, the last two on an unpaved dirt road. I wanted very much to visit the Murchison Falls National Park – the huge, wild expanse of forest around the falls of the Nile. Sure, the area had been repeatedly attacked by the rebels of the Lord's Resistance Army (LRA), but somehow I just counted

on us being lucky. When the only white people we met on the road, people who had lived in the area for several years, emphatically warned us against visiting the park, I eventually became just a bit uneasy. We had already booked our trip. And the Jeep. Jutta was not exactly happy with the situation …

In the simple grass hut with the clay floor – best not to leave it at night, because of the lions – nights were very loud, as nights in the bush just are, and we were uneasy, as is often the case when the chance that one might be kidnapped by rebels while one is trying to sleep is any value above zero per cent. But somehow things went well this time, yet again, and we were given the gift of some days of adventure in the enchantingly beautiful wilderness of East Africa. And after these days between the rapids of the Nile, the tall savannah grass, crocodiles, hippos and many antelopes, we began our bumpy drive back to the mission centre from which we had started our trip.

Back in the Emmaus Centre in Katikamu, our first night in a bed! But it ends loudly – interrupted early by what one might call 'praise'. And what praise actually is, is something I only really learned in Africa. Never again would I underestimate how important it is for prayer.

As I said, it starts loud. And it stays that way: the band begins a few minutes before the planned start at 6am. A drummer, bass, electric guitar, various other drums and singers. I immediately notice that the guitar is badly out of tune. And it is so loud that it doesn't need an amplifier. The kid playing it is maybe ten. The drummer appears to think he should hit as many drums and cymbals as possible with each beat. And a mixture of young and old sing, bellow and hoot at the top of their lungs along with it. But that's not all! There's dancing! And I mean real dancing – maximum motion of as many limbs as possible. In spite of heat. And amidst it all: radiant smiles and enthusiastic clapping.

The joy of African praise is contagious. It is neither forced nor in need of a long warm-up. It is already there at 6am and it continues for more than an hour. Boisterous praise quickly comes under suspicion in Germany: are people being emotionally manipulated? Isn't this superficial and maybe even dangerous? We rapidly forget that we only slap '*Verboten*'[13] on such uninhibited joy in our church services; in the football stadium or at a dance club it is astonishingly normal. But God is really supposed to have a problem with our enthusiasm?

Once I'm back in Germany, my heart feels like it's caught a cold. The mood here is so much more closed and gloomy. I miss the broad smiles of our African friends, the way their faces light up with joy. I miss the enthusiasm. I just miss Africa. And even though a vast horde of giant red ants had tried to set up home in our bed during our last night in Mbarara, and even though we came within a hair's breadth of missing our flights both in Entebbe and then again in Dubai – yes, I had been a bit too optimistic in my planning again – we come back from Africa with a longing for such joy in praise.

THE LRA, AIDS AND PRAYER

But anyone who sees only the joy in Africa has a romanticized picture of the continent. If you scratch the surface even a little, in many places you can see the gaping wounds of history. Everywhere we went people told us of the atrocities of the rebel army, the LRA, and its demonic leader, Joseph Kony. We heard the stories of the horrific events everywhere in the neighbouring countries: Sudan, Congo, Rwanda. And Uganda itself lived through a series of dictatorships in the seventies and eighties that claimed hundreds of thousands of lives. Beautiful as the African countryside can be, warm as the African people can be, her conflicts are unimaginably bloody. Child soldiers, rapes, mass executions …

The Christians here, however, had a different story to tell: one of fasting and prayer. In the middle of a total crisis, a movement of repentance suddenly broke out. Christians had gathered everywhere, even across denominational boundaries, and had begun to beseech God for a change in their country. People gathered in churches and in the jungle to pray. Constantly. And apparently God answered. In

13 German word for 'forbidden'.

fact, Uganda began to experience increasing economic consolidation and political stability in the late nineties. Churches were growing everywhere. But the most astonishing development was this: fewer and fewer people were contracting AIDS, even though Uganda had, for some time, been one of the worst-afflicted countries.

Everywhere people told us of signs and wonders of God: one Christian, a member of the free church in the capital city of Kampala, told us of several hundred medically confirmed healings from AIDS. A taxi driver told us that, although he was admittedly illiterate, he was responsible for seventeen prayer groups. Everywhere we went people related countless experiences in the battle against the Devil and demons. In fact, both light and darkness seemed to be especially visible in Africa: the miracles and the massacres. In both of these, though, something proved itself again and again, and in extraordinary ways, something which fascinates me more and more: the power of persistent prayer. And in Uganda this even showed itself across denominational boundaries. So in autumn 2003, I scratched what I dreamed of onto a piece of paper: a house with a burning heart inside. A heart that burned incessantly, day and night.

BETWEEN TWO WORLDS

Munich, May 2004
The search for 'the New' and 'the More' continues. Since 1999 I have been studying to be a high school teacher of German and religion at the Ludwig Maximilians University in Munich. At the start I also took a lot of Hebrew and then, increasingly, courses in philosophy. That I then add a Masters in theology as part of my double major is a coincidence. Unfortunately, I find most of it boring. My great love is, more and more, literary studies, linguistics and philosophy. The infectious joy of research and the radical, questioning nature of these subjects stand in a painful contrast to the dull churchy navel-gazing that I encounter in most theology departments (naturally there are also exceptions). I am caught between two worlds.

Analytical and postmodern philosophy fascinate me intellectually, with their scalpel-sharp criticism questioning everything. Yet I usually spend the mornings with an hour of personal prayer and in reading the works of Teresa of Avila. And by now I am working all over Germany in the 'Youth Outreach of the Catholic Charismatic Renewal', where there are regular meetings of dozens, sometimes hundreds of teenagers in various places. And then comes theology … but there is a cry for something else inside me. Of course I love Jesus. I love his church, from which I have received so much that is wonderful. And yet there is this intellectual dissatisfaction that causes me to question so much, and later leads to my dissertation 'Metaphorical Theology'. And this dissatisfaction with the rigidity of the forms of faith. Everything in this colourful city and everything in our vibrant youth meetings cries out for living and celebrating the Gospel in all of its sharpness and beauty in a new, different way. But how? I sense that I am standing between two worlds and something new has to begin …

These are brilliant, wild and lovely years in Munich. Newly married and living in a tiny flat in a bad part of town. My hair is blue. During the day I put minimal effort into my university studies, which makes it possible to continue my work with the youth ministry and maintain my prayer life. Evenings I get standing room spots at the opera and listen to Wagner's works. Wagner and Derrida. Richard Rorty and John of the Cross. I ask myself if this is what postmodern life feels like …

THE FIRST MIRACLES

At night I traverse the alternative clubs in the electro-scene with friends. And we talk about Jesus. We are interested in the new, the dangerous, the radical. The experience from 1999 that I mentioned? I've never forgotten it. It left a permanent longing in me. And now we have heard about Heidi Baker in Mozambique and about completely implausible-sounding signs and wonders. In the light of believable reports (and in the end I will get to know the reporter personally!)

of resurrections from the dead in the name of Jesus, some of the statements from historical-critical exegesis lose their credibility for me. Naturally we begin to pray for healings, freedom and prophetic words ourselves. We begin to talk to people on the street spontaneously, to set our course based on prophetic impressions and to experience God's working in person. Hearing every morning in my seminar that the reports of healing in the New Testament are only to be understood symbolically, when one repeatedly sees miracles every afternoon and evening, puts some distance between me and academic theology that I will never really bridge.

We want to see God's working first hand. Before one youth camp, we begin a twenty-one-day fast, praying through a whole night. I will not forget the incredible quantities of espresso, the tired but radiant eyes of this holy conspiracy of new initiates and, most of all, the enchantment of the new, when it was finally morning.

We do street evangelism with our prayer group at Munich Main Station. We pray for people, give out tea and cookies to homeless people and talk about Jesus with them. Wonderful experiences with a God who blesses our clumsy steps again and again. But the most comical, if not the simplest of these actions was one we named 'Face Your Fears'. This meant, simply: do something, even though you are afraid ... although they were not exactly the apex of maturity and wisdom, these crazy missions were important lessons on a path into a new liberty.

SPITTING IN THE FACE OF THE FEAR OF MAN

Somewhere in a train, July 2004
I sit down in a train compartment and decide to pray, because I have not yet had my prayer time today. So, I close my eyes and try to think about God. Suddenly this thought occurs: 'Strange. At home you always kneel when you pray!' I push the distraction aside and try, again, to concentrate. But the thought does not go away. First, my mind tells me: 'There are four people sitting in this compartment, among them a soldier, a cute young girl, and a

respectable businessman, in his prime ... what would they think if you were to kneel before them? And what would you gain?' There are so many good reasons *not* to do it. And yet: didn't Resi and I have a pact not to let ourselves be intimidated in such situations, but to 'spit in the face of the fear of man' instead? I think about it, going back and forth. Ultimately the tension becomes almost unendurable. I stand up and go to the bathroom. When I walk out of the compartment, I see that we are at the very front of the train. A young man with a relaxed expression is coming out of the bathroom as I approach. A young man wearing a black T-shirt adorned with a red devil complete with trident. 'Aha!', I think. And only now do I become aware of the bizarre contradiction of it all! Here we sit in the front of the train and a fan of the greatest loser of all time is not afraid to run around with an image of this loser on his T-shirt. Meanwhile the friend of God, of the absolute winner, is ashamed of himself. Afraid to show his colours, of admitting that he belongs to the greatest winner of all time!

At this point I just shut the thought process down (it helps sometimes) and do that which I had been wanting to do all along. I open the compartment door, kneel down on the floor (my head is only about a foot from the knee of the man sitting across from me) and close my eyes. I can literally feel the eyes of my fellow passengers, their indignation, on me. To be honest, my prayer is perhaps five minutes long and not the most reverent ever. But when I stand up, I am filled with the joyful awareness that I have just 'spat in the face of the fear of man'. I cast a friendly, smiling glance around the group and notice that none of them risks meeting my eye: one is staring out the window, one at his newspaper and the other at the floor. So what! Gradually the passengers disembark at their stops and, when I am finally alone there, I rejoice inside: it was so much easier than I had thought it would be. Yeah, nothing really happened. 'Fear of man will prove to be a snare' (Proverbs 29:25), and it liberates my heart to resist it. Many similar situations follow.

At some point it becomes really 'in' among some of my friends to tell each other about when and how we had punched the fear of man in the face. Sharing about Jesus in a witchcraft shop, talking to drunk punks, laying hands on and praying for a sick Muslim lady on an airplane … All of this does not really have to turn into a kind of sport (but overcoming fear costs something, you bet!), but it becomes a natural expression of a truth we consider self-evident: I am a child of God and as such I am free. Or as Jesus said: 'I do not accept glory from human beings' (John 5:41). A liberating and magnificent lifestyle. A lifestyle that is going to shape the steps toward the Augsburg House of Prayer, where we live out of the confidence that even the most apparently unusual decisions make sense even if they completely contradict human common sense.

The first victories over the fear of man … the memory of these first small exercises still strengthens me years later, when fear of man still tries to make inroads, telling me that true safety lies in the good opinion of man. But the truth is: at the end of my life I'm going to stand before a throne. And on that day there is only one opinion about me that will count. Not that of my neighbours, not that of my colleagues, only that of the one who is seated on that throne and whose eyes are like flames of fire (Revelation 1:14).

An attitude that is important day after day in prayer: I consciously place myself under his gaze, and not under the gaze of men.

STOKING THE FIRE

A short exercise: we are under the eyes of man practically every minute of our day. These can be people who are actually present: in the subway, the glances and gazes of others light on me. What are they thinking? Do I look good? The eyes of the boss or colleagues: am I good enough? They can also be the 'eyes' of people who are not even physically present: what would my mother think, if she saw what a mess my room is? The eyes of my own 'inner judge' can be just as hard to bear as those of people who are really present.

In prayer, we leave the gaze of man and come under the gaze of God. That is not easy, because we are accustomed to living a life in the fear of man. We want to be liked. The way of Jesus, however, is a radically different one. It leads to a life that is completely under God's gaze. In prayer we can practise this foundational attitude that then gradually leavens our entire life.

Sit down in a quiet place. Close your eyes and try to identify under whose gaze you are living. Whose expectations, whose opinions, whose judgements do you feel? Take time for these questions and scrutinize them very carefully: do you want to keep living under these? You have an invitation. And it comes from your loving Father. He asks: 'Would you rather live entirely under my gaze? My gaze sets you free and in it you will find your dignity and beauty.'

Make a decision and inwardly walk out of the gaze of others and into the gaze of the Father. You can imagine it as a cone of light or a ray of warm sunlight falling on your skin on a day at the beach. More important than whether a certain feeling that can be linked with it, or not, is the inner act of your heart. 'Lord, I want to live under your gaze. Lord, I want to give you this prayer time and be before your eyes alone.' These little decisions will gradually have a lasting effect on your everyday life.

THE CALL
One Hundred per Cent Prayer

IN THE INTERNATIONAL HOUSE OF PRAYER

Kansas City, USA, June 2005
The adventure that will lead to the Augsburg House of Prayer continues. In the autumn of 2003, a few days after I first drew the little symbol of a house with a burning heart, I met someone who told me about the 'International House of Prayer', an inter-confessional prayer centre in the USA, directed by Mike Bickle.

The name was not entirely new to me; the first spiritual book that I ever bought for myself was *Passion for Jesus*,[14] which Mike had written. I was fifteen, and it had a lasting impact on me. Now I hear about this astonishing place where praise never stops, day or night. After some toing and froing, it's decided: we're going to Kansas! Due to fortunate circumstances we are even able to meet the leadership team at IHOPKC. But what are we supposed to do there for three weeks? Jutta is especially put off by the thought of being surrounded for hours and hours by loud music. And we are not free of our own prejudices: don't these free-churchers always shout when they pray? Isn't all of this Protestant noise just a superficial, American show?

Somehow, we have to survive our time in the USA.

The decision is made quickly: a week in New York has to be in the schedule too, meaning there will be just two weeks in Kansas.

New York is, of course, unforgettable. We arrive late in the evening – a full year old, Samuel slept through the flight. We wait at the luggage counter: Jutta's luggage is lost. Completely exhausted, we arrive at the youth hostel in Manhattan. It's tropically hot. Then Samuel wakes up. So, I prowl around Midtown with him at night. A tuna salad sandwich and a beer in a 24/7-deli. Over the following

---

14 Mike Bickle, *Passion for Jesus*, (Charisma House, 1994).

days we visit the Museum of Modern Art, Ground Zero and the Metropolitan Museum of Art. And we are excited about Kansas; surely there's a lot to see there, too. The shock hits us pretty hard when we get there. There is in fact *absolutely nothing* interesting to see in Kansas City. And for miles around just flat land, endless suburban streets ... really nothing interesting. Just a place where people pray, and have been praying non-stop for nearly six years ...

Our first experiences at IHOPKC are less spectacular than I expected. We are in the prayer room a lot in the mornings, and in the afternoons I play with our little Samuel and talk with Jutta about what we have experienced. Yet somehow the impressions have a lasting effect on us. The devotion of several hundred (!) staff who keep prayer going day and night impresses us. Nothing about it seems exaggerated, put-on or manipulated. It all feels like a natural expression of their love for Jesus. I am overwhelmed by the selection in their bookstore: here I find Bernard of Clairvaux, Hans Urs von Balthasar and all of the classics of spiritual life. As a Catholic, I had often been put off by the theological and spiritual 'flatness' of many Protestant and Charismatic groups. But here I see a respect for the great traditions and yet so much courage to try something wholly new.

I am shown a great deal of respect (especially by the leadership), which is not something to be assumed if one considers my Catholic background. The connection between prayer and theological training (IHOPKC has its own Bible school) makes a deep impression on me. But, at least initially, nothing more. Jutta and I pray every day, and in fact it is Jutta who is the first of us to say, 'Johannes, I have the impression that we should do something like this in Germany. And you should do it full time.' As the stronger visionary of the two of us, I feel like I have been passed on the right by my otherwise so down-to-earth wife. I quarrel for a few days. Suddenly the very thought I have already been half-consciously living towards for some years seems so radical. But the real explosion comes from Andy and the canoe.

SHARDS AND THE RESURRECTION OF THE DEAD

I register for a seminar that's supposed to be about prophecy. Admittedly, I learn very little about it on this Saturday, but it still changes my life forever. Not bad at all for a ten-dollar seminar fee ...

There he is: Andy, thirty-one. He comes from New Zealand and is a substitute teacher for the man who was supposed to actually lead the seminar. At first, the seminar deals generally with Biblical prophecy. Very nice. In my mind I go through Dostoyevsky's *The Brothers Karamazov*, which I've been reading on the trip. In the second part, though, Andy begins to tell us about his life. About his absolutely radical conversion, which resulted in the conversion of his whole family (his father's a missionary now). And he tells us how God started talking to him. At the time he had a small company that did glass repairs, fixing broken windows and doors. At one point he decided to stop simply waiting until he received a call for a job, but instead started to ask God, 'Lord, where should I go today?' – and just take off. Sometime during the day he would get a call: 'Could you please come, my window is broken. I live at this address in so-and-so street'. Andy would answer, 'No problem, madam, I'm already parked in front of your house.' And he would use the improbability of his spontaneous arrival and the shards of the window lying around as a chance to tell the woman of the house about Jesus, who still speaks today and makes the broken whole, even in the heart.

Sounds unbelievable? It did to me, too. But Andy does not stop telling these stories – he tells one after the other. The high point is his report of how he was used by God to raise the dead. That's right. Raise the dead. Jesus in fact commissions his disciples to do things like this (Matthew 10:8) and we are familiar with such events from church history. But really?

His narrative is completely credible: Andy was witness to a horrible motorcycle accident. The young man's skull was horribly crushed, no pulse. The doctor said he couldn't do any more. Andy prayed – as he says – the 'weakest prayer of my life' without any feeling of special authority: 'Live in Jesus' name!' and touched him on the shoulder. At that moment the young man drew a deep breath and came back to life. He was evacuated from the scene in a helicopter and to the amazement of the doctors he was released from the hospital, completely healed, after a few days.

Now at last he had aroused my interest, this Andy. And my question was: what is his secret? And what does all this mean for me?

DEEPER THAN LONG

Andy explains how the written word of God and the heard, prophetic word of God are closely connected. Ultimately, it's the same God who speaks. The written word of God must always be the measure of every prophetic word. But he has discovered that he hears more from God, and more clearly, if he loves his written word and 'digests' it. For this reason, he arranged with some friends to meditate on the same verse of a Psalm, for four hours every day.

What?! Four hours?!

He says it with the casual assurance of someone reading a recipe: 'just four hours or so in the oven'. Anyhow, he explained how he operated: just one verse. Praying this verse and slowly ruminating on it. Praying it back to God, reformulating it as a personal prayer. And singing. And writing it down. And repeating it over and over again. Four hours long. Yes, he has learned that the word is much deeper than it is long. Even short verses have true dimensions of depth and hidden stories of spiritual truth.

Okay, until now I thought I knew the Bible well and had an ardent spiritual life. But I had never heard of such a thing. The shock hits me hard when Andy's suggestion hammers home. 'Yeah, and every three weeks we start another verse.' After I pick my jaw up from the floor and shove my eyes back in my head, I'm still stunned. Three weeks, four hours a day, *one* verse?! This shows a true love for the word of God, a deep knowledge and a determination to put it into action that just leaves me speechless. And no wonder it is producing fruit that I've never heard of before!

THE CANOE

At the end of the seminar each person is meant to receive prophetic words from the others. Everyone gets something nice – everyone but me. I am the only one left. Andy prays for me and immediately gets a picture. And this little picture from 17 June 2005 changes everything. It shows Samuel, Jutta and me standing on a bridge. The bridge extends over a long, straight river that is lined with trees left and right. A canoe is floating under the bridge and the Lord says, 'it's time to jump into the canoe'. From above, everything looks like a crossroads.

At first, I don't know what to make of it. But Jutta and I return to the picture again and again in prayer, and we sense that we are approaching a crossroads in our lives. Does this confirm Jutta's vision, and is founding a House of Prayer the canoe we're supposed to jump into? A bit shaky and unsteady, but fast and agile: that's what a daring new project could feel like – like a canoe.

We only become aware of the whole weight of this image about two years later. At first the canoe picture is our divine 'go-ahead' to get things started with the House of Prayer that we had been dreaming about for so long. And for months the word 'canoe' remains a synonym for us for the House of Prayer. We want to cast off in our canoe. With Veronika, Sebastian, Tom, Raphael, Theresa, Bas and Julia (many of whom I have already known for years through youth ministry) we have a team who are soon on board with us, and today they are all pillars of the Augsburg House of Prayer.

In the beginning, we don't tell anyone that Jutta and I have made a firm decision to found a House of Prayer. We tell people only about what we have experienced at IHOPKC, and we decide to gather to us all who spontaneously respond with, 'I want to be part of something like that'. We don't want to generate any hype, just to have people with us whose hearts are already burning for the same thing. One weekend in August 2005 we light the touchpaper and tell everyone about our canoe plans.

ON THE BRIDGE

Initially it is entirely unclear where the House of Prayer is supposed to be established. For a year and half we meet as a group – a group that is constantly growing – in various places in southern Germany, and we pray for direction, for where we should be. At the first 'Experience Prayer Summits', possessing drive yet lacking sleep, we make our first attempt to hold prayer and worship sessions for a few days at a time. Glorious first steps! By December 2005, through this spiritual reflection several members of our group have received the impression that Augsburg is the right city for the House of Prayer. It moves me particularly because of its ecumenical significance: it was here that Luther had to answer to Cardinal Cajetan. It was here that the actual break between the Lutheran movement and Rome happened. But the first religious peace treaty was concluded here in 1555, and in 1999 the Joint Statement on the Doctrine of Justification was signed here. Augsburg seems to have a significant inheritance – which includes both painful episodes as well as glorious ones. I only find out later that Augsburg was once the centre of global finance.

Firstly, I contact the Diocesan Office to ask if we would be welcome there. The Twelve Apostles Parish (*Zwölf Apostel*) in Augsburg's Hochzoll district is suggested as an ideal point of contact, and we are told that we would, indeed, be welcomed. Once I complete my doctoral thesis and our daughter, Anna, has been born, Jutta and I begin to look around for a flat in Augsburg. Our budget is not very big; we are already living 'by faith'. The second flat we look at is affordable and perfectly suited for us: after having looked all over the city, to our amazement it is only a few metres from the Twelve Apostles church. But the truly big surprise comes only a few days later as we take a walk around the area: the river Lech flows very near the flat, and there is a canoe racing course right there that was built for the 1972 Olympics in Munich. The Canoe World Cup races are still held there. And here we are. A little family all together on a bridge with a long canoe racing course right in front of us, trees to the left and right. And just then a canoe floats past under the bridge. *We're standing in Andy's prophetic picture!* God could not have made the location clearer to us. Astonished at the wisdom of God's leadership, we just look at each other. It still takes a while before I find out that there are already three different groups in Augsburg who are praying for an Augsburg House of Prayer, and who have had 24-hour prayer on their hearts. Some of them are startled that a Catholic couple, of all people, are really starting one, but the ways of the Lord are sometimes as full of twists and turns as a journey in a canoe.

After this, everything happens rather quickly. With friends and fellow-travellers, we try out 24-hour prayer more and more often. We trial it during a Conference of the Charismatic Renewal, where we set up a prayer room with great zeal, organize alternating teams with worship leaders, listen to God, store up energy drinks and feel like a spiritual special forces unit.

The first evening I take a walk in Fulda. Fulda is my wife's hometown. Fulda – in the heart of Germany. And Fulda is the place where St. Boniface is buried, the first great missionary to come to Germany. There is a question burning inside me: what has to happen to bring revival to this country?

There, in the Cathedral Square in Fulda, an image appears before my mind's eye. It's like a vision, a film in my head, and it makes me aware of how significant these small beginnings we have made really are.

Black everywhere. Ruins. Shattered walls reach upward into the sky. A bombed-out city. Smoking rubble and scorched earth. Black birds circle. The smell of decay and corpses in the air. A despairing image of complete hopelessness. An image of death. Suddenly I see a small group of young people. There aren't many. Maybe seven, maybe twelve. They are standing in a circle. In the middle of the smoking rubble, in the middle of this devastation. They look weak and naïve. Young, inexperienced and insignificant. But they begin to sing. They stand in the wreck of this destroyed city and they sing. The song is quiet ... and at first nothing seems to move. But then the wind begins to stir at the sound of this song. A gentle breeze rises and drives away the stench of corpses. The vultures fly off and the atmosphere appears to change. Everything is still in ruins and yet the scene is changing.

Very slowly, but constantly ... and far away in the distance, the sky opens up and a stream of bright, orange light penetrates the dark, leaden cloud cover. And in the middle of the night: a song. A small, constant song that seems so insignificant and yet changes everything.

STEPS ON THE WATER

Bank machine, Schellingstraße, Munich, September 2006
I print out my account statement and ask myself, 'What is God going to think of to get me and my family through this month?' A lot has happened: the House of Prayer vision is taking on a clearer shape and my dissertation is almost complete. In August my little contract with the university runs out, and as of now we are officially living – still without regular supporters – 'by faith'. We are expecting our second (third) child and live in a small flat, with bad gas heating, that costs over 800 euros a month. We are depending on God, but he has already dramatically proven that we can trust him.

My first little book has already been published, and I am being paid for some of my speaking engagements. Financing my full-time commitment as an intercessor from these earnings seems a very justified hope.

And then, suddenly, comes the gnawing thought: what would happen if I didn't keep this money, but instead only lived from donor support?

The very concept seems absurd: I don't have an income, and now I am also supposed to give away what I do get – that's not a plan with a promising future for my young family! And yet the thought does not leave. I concede to at least keep touching on it in prayer.

That same week I am approached at the university and told that – of all the many employees – I am to receive a bonus from the remaining funds in the budget for the professorial chair. The amount mentioned is around 500 euros! Then, on the Wednesday evening I am invited to the home of some friends – I am giving them advice about their website. When they push 100 euros in my direction at the end of our time together, I am really astonished. But on Friday my astonishment reaches its apex: I am supposed to pick up the lasagne that a woman who runs a restaurant has prepared for our youth weekend. It has happened over and over again that people give me small contributions for our youth ministry, so I am not completely surprised when the hostess opens her purse and says, 'I want to give you something!' Then her fingers suddenly grab a big, thick roll of bills and she hands it to me with the words, 'God told me I am supposed to give this to you, and not for the youth ministry, but for you and your family!'

My jaw almost hits the floor. Of course, just like my colleague and my friends from Wednesday evening, she knows nothing about my planning to live 'by faith'. And there is certainly no way any of them can know that I am wondering whether God would provide for us if I were to give away all of the money that I earn from books, CDs and public speaking engagements … Yet the hostess just gave me about 600 euros – and in 48 hours I have seen first-hand how God can provide my month's salary. And this happens before I have really stepped into this lifestyle completely. It is like having the gold ring and bouquet of roses for the bride before even proposing to her.

This is an offer I can't refuse. And God has been faithful ever since. All of my earnings from teaching, songs and media flow right back into the kingdom of God, one hundred per cent. Meanwhile, God has provided for me and my growing family to this very day, constantly (and through our many kind supporters) so that we have never had a shortfall. Again and again the water bears the feet of those who take their steps in faith.

Indeed, the life of prayer is always a life of trust in God's provision. Jesus tells us, 'Do not worry,' and, 'Ask in faith,' practically in the same breath. Yes – prayer is inseparable from the faithful confidence that there is divine provision. In our own life as a family we have seen this again and again, and we continue to see it. Even now with four children, and all the inevitable expenses associated with that we, like the entire staff of the House of Prayer, live wholly from support. And God is so faithful in providing for us that we don't even have impressive stories of heroic acts of faith. He provides before we find ourselves in dire need. Prayer teaches faith, tangibly, like in trusting God for your income. I have experienced this many, many times.

THE SCANDAL OF PRAYER

In early 2007 the adventure finally begins: a life wholly given to prayer. With my heart on fire, I wrote the following lines, reproduced here unedited. They were written immediately after we had traded our lovely student flat in Munich for one in a block of flats on the edge of Augsburg:

Recently I have been asked, quite often, what I do for a living. Somehow word has got out that I have completed my university studies. And then the question is unavoidable: 'And have you found a job yet?' At this point I find myself confronted again and again with the difficult decision of choosing the easy response or the more difficult one. There are two options for presenting our vision for a House of Prayer:

Option A: The House of Prayer is to be a place where people pray around the clock. People can come in to recharge – a spiritual oasis, so to speak. It will also be a place where we train young people, mostly, to grow in their spiritual lives and their character.

Option B: The House of Prayer shall be a place where we pray around the clock. This means capable young people like me will spend the majority of their time sitting in a room and talking to God. This primarily serves God alone, since there usually won't be any visitors there. And it costs a whole lot of money.

Which is closer to reality? Option A has a lot of truth in it. As a matter of fact, all kinds of good things do happen when we pray. People will recharge in our prayer room, will get healed and will get training. Revival will come (I am firmly convinced). But that does not really get to the heart of our calling. Our real calling is to be there for God alone. And that is offensive to some. Christianity is fully acceptable, socially, as long as it is just a form of pious social service ministry, or when it comes to standing for certain values and a certain set of ethics. Or if it's part of your personal spiritual search. That's all fine. But wanting to be there 'just for God' – that's offensive.

The following statements are true:

I am twenty-eight, have a family to feed, a doctorate, and I spend the majority of my time talking to God.

I have deliberately decided not to pursue a normal career because I want to pray instead.

I have a vision for many people doing the same thing and supporting themselves through donations.

And what's the point of it all? I think it's worth leading such a life because Jesus is worth it. And even if revival does not come, no one comes to visit and no one sees or hears what we do, I still think that wasting my life for him is not a waste.

At this point it really gets offensive. Why? Because the fact that there are people whose primary goal in life is to talk with God confronts us with the hidden atheism in our own hearts; the hidden atheism in our hearts, our culture – and our church. What do I mean by that?

Prayer is important. But does it need to be the main activity in anyone's life?

Prayer is important. But whom does it benefit if it does not result in action or people aren't inspired by it?

Prayer is important. But should anyone really pay for people to do nothing but that?

Prayer is important. But we need every volunteer for the event we're planning. We are happy to pray before we start, but we need to prioritize 'practical' help over prayer. We can't spare anyone who would invest hours or even days just praying for the event.

Prayer is important. But when it comes to the problems of our society, our church or my company, I'd rather depend on my own common sense.

Prayer is so offensive because it seems like capitulation. The man who prays admits that he is at the end of his resources. 'Trouble teaches you to pray,' as we say here in Germany. And quite often the only guy who prays is the one who's in trouble.

Our world is saturated with a lie, and this lie says that we are the captains of our fate. You can read statements in any number of books which imply that, because people in earlier times did not have the ability to fight disease with medicine, they believed in supernatural powers. The inventor of modern exegesis, Rudolf Bultmann, said: 'We cannot use electric lights and radios and, in the event of illness, avail ourselves of modern medical and clinical means and at the same time believe in the spirit and wonder world of the New Testament'.[15]

We go to the doctor if we are sick. We build early warning systems to deal with earthquakes. If a land is suffering from poverty, The UN will help. If families fall apart, it's often up to the state to provide social support. If the church runs out of money, parishes are consolidated. If the climate changes, politicians meet to deal with it. If there's an increase in neo-Nazism in Germany, we start programmes in the schools to combat it. There is one thought behind all of this that holds the Western world firmly in its grip, so firmly that we have stopped noticing: all things are possible for man. We have got used to thinking our lives are in our hands alone and that we can solve any problem with a bit of goodwill and persistence. But this way of thinking defies reality:

Only young, healthy people really control their lives. But many are old, sick or handicapped. They are constantly confronted with the fact that they are not in control of their lives, but are dependent on others. And those young, healthy people of today will someday be old and sick.

We only really control a very small part of our lives. We can't choose what bodies we have. We also cannot choose who our fellow humans are. Nor can we choose random events, the weather and the economy. And these things shape our lives.

We are only in control of ourselves to a certain degree. What guarantee is there that I'm not going to wake up tomorrow with depression or total burn-out? And what guarantee is there for my spouse or my children?

And we definitely are not in control of all social developments

15 Rudolf Bultmann, *New Testament and Mythology and Other Basic Writings*, translated by Schubert Ogden, (Fortress Press, 1984).

around us. Both World Wars were anticipated and feared by millions of people – and yet they were not prevented.

We are not in control of our deaths. The moment of death is the most total and complete negation of all thought of human autonomy. Everyone is going to die, and no one knows when. And no one has any influence over it.

Praying means recognizing one's own helplessness. Only someone who is helpless asks for help. And the truth is we are helpless. We only have control over a relatively small part of our lives, our society, our church, our family. And in respect to the most urgent human problems, no human has any really effective solutions. The following questions are important to millions of people, and there are no convincing human answers to them:

How can a person change his basic nature (if he is an egomaniac, constant complainer, liar, adulterer or rapist)?

How does a person make peace with his past and heal his inner wounds?

What will rescue families and marriages, truly and sustainably?

What really brings purpose and fulfilment in life?

How can a nation, or the youth culture, be changed for the better?

Someone who prays admits that he does not have the solutions to offer for mankind's problems. Of course, it's not a flight from responsibility – quite the opposite: someone who prays feels more keenly responsible than anyone else. And to be an intercessor does not mean that one devalues action and faithful work. But our world is bewitched by the lie that it can change *everything* through work, good ideas and money. But this is not so. Ultimately only God can change the human heart. And the one who prays is confessing faith in God. He confesses that he *only* has faith in God.

The contemplative orders were always a thorn in the flesh of the world. Because withdrawing into a monastery in the desert and singing Psalms makes no sense according to human standards. It makes just as little sense to convince people to sing songs and continue in intercession around the clock. *In fact, it's absolutely pointless if there is no God!*

Doing it at all assumes *a priori* that God *does* exist. And he is worthy of being loved for his own sake. Wasting one's life in prayer – whether in the case of the Carmelites in the thirteenth century or today in the Augsburg House of Prayer – witnesses to this truth with every breath, with every hour, that whoever loses their life for Jesus' sake 'will save it', and 'whoever wants to save their life will lose it' (Luke 9:24). The one given to prayer confesses what the Second Vatican Council also confessed, that 'man, who is the only creature on earth which God willed for itself, cannot fully find himself except through a sincere gift of himself' (*Gaudium et spes 25*).

Of course, not everyone is called to such a lifestyle. Indeed, it's few who are. Nevertheless, whenever someone asks, 'Your job is talking to God, really?' You should answer:

'Yes!'

'And you want others to do the same thing?'

'Exactly!'

'And what does it do?'

'Well, nothing. At all! It accomplishes nothing at all and it does nothing for anyone. Which is why it accomplishes everything. For everyone.'

STOKING THE FIRE

Frequently people ask me what one can do to start a prayer group, a House of Prayer, or to find a worship team. Or how one could change an existing church or group. My experience tells me it is difficult even to lead the horse to water, let alone encourage it to drink. Making progress with people who really don't want 'more', or don't want anything different, usually just exhausts both parties. I would simply look for like-minded people in an existing group whose hunger is already awakened, taking care not to split the group but to create different spaces for different focuses. I would start with a small group of people who share this longing of the heart, and begin regular prayer. Once the fire is durably cultivated in a small group (which must carefully guard itself against the critical urge and arrogance towards others!), there is the chance that more and more people will be attracted to the fire, and the whole church or ministry will be drawn in. Strictly speaking, at the very beginning it's unimportant whether large numbers of people come. Indeed, at first it's often better with a group of only two or three who share clarity and vision! What burns on a small scale for a long time, God will bless with visible growth. That is my firm conviction.

Therefore, look for one or two comrades-in-arms and start small. If you can't find anyone local, then look farther afield. But you can also pray by Skype or telephone and then meet occasionally – maybe for an entire Saturday. Make a courageous start!

DISSONANCE
Prayer and Pain

GREAT LIGHT AND GREAT PAIN

Maistraße, Munich, November 2005
I sit here in a grey corridor and stare out at the snow-covered back courtyard. Beds are wheeled past; the hours advance relentlessly. I sit here and struggle to grasp what's just happened.

The year 2005 is, for me, inseparably linked with a nearly unbearable dissonance between God's power and great suffering. It's a dissonance that many people, the good and great included, have had to face again and again.

In the summer of 2004, our first child, Samuel, was born. Our nights got shorter, our lives so much richer. Our joy, then, was even greater when a year later Jutta told me that we were going to become parents again. On the very same evening that we told our friends we wanted to found a House of Prayer, we also told them about our second child. The events surrounding the little House of Prayer plant were getting more and more exciting, and in the meantime, I was still writing my doctoral thesis. Professor Neuner had even made it possible for me to have a minor paid position associated with his professorial chair.

It's often in a single minute that your life changes forever. One such minute hit me hard on 25 November 2005. My phone rang. A terrified Jutta was on the line, asking me to come home. She was bleeding and had to get to the hospital immediately. We found a babysitter for Samuel, and before long were at the Women's Hospital in *Maistraße*. The diagnosis: ascending infection, acute danger to our child. Our child: our son Simon, whom we already know from ultrasound images and his first movements in the abdomen, whom we lovingly call 'Simsim'. Our son, whose life I now fear for as I sit in a grey corridor and wait.

Everything began to happen so quickly. The infection puts Jutta in danger. The doctors say we should consider an abortion. Life has altered completely. We were used to the security of our regular, everyday existence, and suddenly we're confronted with options that threaten to change the course of our lives. Strict bed rest until the birth would keep me at home for months, bringing all other activities to a halt. Our child could be handicapped for life. And Jutta herself is in danger from this infection; what if it leaves her sterile? What if it even becomes life-threatening? Praying is all we can do now. We immediately decide against an abortion. Our only option, medically, is high doses of antibiotics. The following days are a mix of fear and hope; they are days of complete uncertainty. When labour pains begin on Thursday evening – in spite of all medical attempts to stop them – I still sense peace in prayer. It seems to me as if the hospital room is full of angels. But have they come to protect Simon, or to escort him to heaven?

FRIDAY

When nothing has changed by the following morning, the doctors insist on rapid action: the child urgently needs to be delivered – not to do so would be too dangerous. Once Jutta is prepared for the surgery and given medication, everything happens extremely quickly. Simon comes into the world right before my eyes: a beautiful, fully-formed baby. But at twenty weeks he is still unable to survive outside of the womb. I don't know whether or not he is alive, but I give him an emergency baptism in the name of the Father, the Son and the Holy Spirit – a baptism which in the Catholic tradition may also be performed by laypeople. My little second-born son lies dead in my hands, his eyes firmly closed. I will never be able to put him to bed, but I lay him on a white towel, surrounded by rapidly wilting flower petals. One day later we carry him to his grave.

We learn an important lesson that day. One of the nurses is a believer and she also knows about our vision for a House of Prayer. She thinks that a vision as great as ours will inevitably come under attack from Satan, and that spiritual warfare will always be aimed at the weakest links in the chain. Simon, she believes, has been a casualty in this war. Yet although this explanation may, in part, be accurate, it's no comfort. When you're suffering, you don't need anyone to explain suffering to you, to search for reasons or rational causes; you just need peace with God and friends who understand it, even if they express their understanding in silence. In truth, suffering can never be completely explained. We live in a world in which not everything that happens is God's will. We live in a world in which innocent children die. Finding peace with God in the midst of this, where every explanation falls short, is not easy, but it is the only hope we have against despair. Even when the pain stays with us.

JUST LET GO, GOD LOVES YOU SO MUCH

Seedorf, Switzerland, August 2012
She walks stooped, leaning on her cane and speaking slowly. And she takes great joy in watching our children play. The only terms of endearment for children she knows are in Swiss German, which she usually switches off when speaking to us. Sister Josefa was once the Mother Superior of a Benedictine Convent. And it is only with some hesitation that she talks about her inner life; one learns not to talk too much about one's mystical experiences. But she still remembers … it was on one Sunday or another in 1972 … right after choral prayer in the afternoon. Yes, that's when it happened.

A little, shrunken woman sits there in her black habit. A woman who has lived all her life simply, rich in poverty, here in a small convent on Lake Lucerne. A woman who has experienced so much more of God than almost anyone I've ever met. Her unfathomable eyes and her sharp gaze from behind her wrinkles reveal more of the depths of God than any book on theology.

Yes … it happened one Sunday in church.

She says she was completely taken up into the Trinity. Submerged in, and united with, the love between the Father, Son and Holy

Spirit. She has never talked about it much before, but my persistent questioning draws more and more out of her.

Yes ... then she just floated on a sea of love for days.

During that time the convent needed to make a decision regarding who was to become Mother Superior. But all that was of no interest to her. Her reality was elsewhere: being in the love of God. It was there that she learned a key aspect in prayer: letting go. Following this realization, her whole life became a single prayer: 'Yes, Lord.' 'Yes,' again and again. Letting go anew, over and over again.

And that remains the main topic throughout all of our discussions and telephone conversations: letting go. Later, Sister Josefa becomes fragile and ill and it is now a great effort for her to write or speak. One day, after she has become bedridden, a younger nun walks in and finds her singing. And what is Josefa singing? A simple melody: 'Just let go. God loves you so much.'

Tears well up in my eyes as this same younger nun recounts the story to the young staff at our House of Prayer. Such a lifetime of wisdom condensed in that prayer! 'Just let go!' A wisdom purified and proven in suffering. Yes, all suffering brings with it the temptation to become bitter. Harder. More disillusioned. And all suffering brings with it the invitation to let go. Let go of some expectations. Let go of the demand for answers to our questions. Finally, to let go of life more and more. And release one's self into the hands of a God who we don't always understand.

Letting go in this way always brings fruit. Suffering will never completely disappear from our lives, but letting go in prayer can make our suffering fruitful. I learned about letting go from Sister Josefa, and I was able to learn about fruitfulness in the shadow of Vesuvius ...

BEAUTY AND PAIN

Caserta, Italy, June 2013
I am serving with Jutta and our youngest daughter, Pauline, in the 'Italia House of Prayer'. Prostitutes line the street for hundreds of metres here in the industrial area of greater Naples, right next to the highway.

Behind it the massive, white volcano is lit up in its evening colours. It is dusk by the time we finally get to the shopping centre where the small House of Prayer has found its, not entirely unimpressive, premises.

I met Giuseppe Conte a year ago at our MEHR Conference (where the leaders of Houses of Prayer from all over Europe gather). He led worship on the piano, Italo-pop Style; his anointing clearly came from a personal relationship with God. There were tears and deep empathy throughout the room as Giuseppe recounted the beginnings, only a few weeks earlier, of the House of Prayer in Caserta: complications had suddenly arisen during the birth of his daughter and, in the space of just a few hours, his wife was dead. Their baby, thankfully, survived. In an upwelling of compassion and faith in a miracle, intercessors and worship leaders from all over Italy gathered at the bed of the woman who had just died. Would God raise her from the dead?

They prayed day and night. This miracle never came … but another one did occur in the dissonance between glory and suffering. There wasn't an hour that day when prayer fell silent – not when the woman lay dying nor after she passed away. And then a question confronted everyone in the room: why stop praying now? And so a vision arose – to let praise to God resound day and night from the heart of Italy.

Jutta and I are filled with a deep reverence, as Catholics in a Catholic country, to have the opportunity of serving these Protestant Christians. They long to see Christians of all denominations come together in constant prayer in the middle of the corruption and prostitution of Naples. The wounds remain, and the tears remain. But God sings his own beautiful song in the midst of the major and minor keys of our lives.

STOKING THE FIRE

What experiences of suffering have you been through in your life? Write them down and invite God into them. Please only take the time to do this if you are going to be completely honest about it. It will most likely mean reliving some of the pain, and even weeping. That's good.

Now, ask yourself when you are praying: Have I really let go of this situation? Please keep in mind that letting go does not mean feeling no more pain. It also does not mean calling what happened 'just', or even 'good'. But it does mean giving God the chance to prove that he is the one who can still make something good, and even beautiful, out of the deepest miseries of human life.

If you are not ready to take this step yet, it is important that you acknowledge this. Don't force yourself into doing it. The time will come when you will sense that freedom and peace lie in letting go. If you are ready, you can express it to God in writing. And maybe an outward gesture will help you too, such as visiting a grave, returning an object, laying a symbolic stone by a roadside shrine, lighting a candle in a church …

THE GREAT JOURNEY
Prayer and Eternity

NOT OF THIS WORLD

Karyes, Mount Athos, Greece, August 2001
He speaks perfect English, even though he looks as though he has just stepped directly out of the Middle Ages, or at least a historical film. And he is one of the first monks we meet on Mount Athos, with just our backpacks and the precious *Diamonitirion* in our pockets – our pilgrimage visa. Up to ten non-Orthodox people may visit this place – the most unusual place in the world – per day. A nation unto itself in the middle of Greece, this eastern-most reach of Halkidiki is only accessible by ship, and only to men. And it consists only of Orthodox monks; there are about 2,000 of them. This thickly forested, nearly primitive mountainous peninsula is unlike any other place in Europe. There are not only no women, but there is no road network, no advertising, no television, not even secular music. It is a place not of this world, a place that follows wholly different laws.

There are no hotels, no restaurants, no meat. Instead there are monasteries. They cling to cliff-sides, crowned with blue domes, skewed like medieval castles, lined with black pines, adorned with wooden balconies. Some are in need of repair, others are lovingly restored. Hundreds of monks live in them and in the many *skiti* (hermitages) on the peninsula. Their lives are dedicated to renunciation and prayer, following the example of others from hundreds of years before. I have visited and explored Athos several times, making pilgrimage from monastery to monastery, sweating and praying.

I will never forget the sounds of Athos: the humming of insects, the murmur of the sea. And in contrast, the silence of the many hours on the small, ancient paths that lead us from one monastery to the next.

The songs. The resounding bells on the censers. The knock on the door in the morning that summons the pilgrim to prayer. The sounding of the tonewood, that takes the place of bells, summoning us to church.

I will never forget the scents of Athos. Most of all, the incense. Lots of incense, with the candles casting their flickering light on the icons in the dark chapels ... And the oil lamps ... And finally, the aromas of the foods of Athos: olives, oily aubergine casserole, coarse bread and strong white wine. And also the inimitable combination of Byzantine mocha, the sharp pomace brandy called *tsipouro*, *loukoumi* (Turkish Delight) and water. Visitors are welcomed with these traditional gifts of hospitality in every monastery.

DEAD TO EVERYTHING

He is the first monk we meet in Karyes. Our conversation is short because we want to reach Philotheou before nightfall: where do we come from? What are our names? We ask the same, and he answers, in perfect English, 'I am from Athos.' OK, this is obvious, so we try to dig a little deeper. We ask where he was born and where he used to live. Perhaps the USA? He simply repeats, 'I am from Athos,' and adds for explanation: 'We have left our earlier lives completely. We died to them and we live a new life here. We don't want to even remember what came before, so that the Devil cannot tempt us through these thoughts.'

This incredibly radical statement jolts us like a bolt of lightning. Here live hundreds of men, young and old, who have not seen their previous homes or their mothers since they arrived. Indeed, the majority of them have not seen any women since they came here! And instead of that life they choose to get up at 2am or 3am every day to pray the 'Jesus Prayer', and then spend several hours participating in the celebration of the Liturgy. They fast on around 200 days a year. Their lives are led more in eternity than on earth.

They wear black cowls as a reminder that they are dead to this world. How strange and yet so instructive! Aren't we Christians all likewise citizens of another world, dead to what is purely earthly? But how little this spiritual truth shapes our normal lives …

The finality of Athos did not intimidate me; it inspired me. Where are the people today who don't see following Jesus simply as a source of help in dealing with their everyday lives, but as a gamble of everything on one single card? Where are the people today who wholly lose themselves in God? And what does this actually mean? This had already become clear to me a few years before this pilgrimage …

ON OVERGROWN PATHS

Qadisha Valley, Lebanon, October 1999
I set off in the early morning. I had spent the night in a storeroom full of old junk, that the local priest generously provided as a place to stay. From Bcharreh, high in the Lebanon mountains, a winding road leads down into the Qadisha Valley. The Holy Valley. Just getting here, hitch-hiking and in shared taxis, has been an adventure. I caught an intestinal infection in Syria, and so I'm not too worried that my provisions are just some dry flatbread and two bananas.

I want to hike through the valley. Qadisha is a canyon, around 40 kilometres long, with sides reaching 200 metres high at the steepest points. Above it, the bare heights of the Lebanon mountains with their majestic cedars. I walk for hours, completely alone. Deeper and deeper into the valley. I don't have a map, but I remember hearing somewhere that there's a path out of the valley back toward Ehden. Abandoned monasteries and hermitages line the path. It looks like it'll be a great day for hiking; I don't yet suspect that I am walking right into a hazardous situation. I hike for hours. At first I enjoy the solitude, but gradually the total desolation of the area begins to get to me and to seem eerie, even threatening. At this point I start wishing for a sign of civilization or another person. Instead, there is wild, primitive nature and a valley that is getting deeper and deeper.

Clouds roll in during the afternoon, the temperature begins to fall and the valley, which is full of deep clefts and chasms, is gradually engulfed in fog. It gets extremely cold, and even after a six-hour march there is no sign of a way out of this canyon. Anywhere. And not only are all the monasteries abandoned and in ruins, but it's been hours since I saw any sign of active human habitation. The cold cuts right through my light cotton clothing and I anxiously calculate that there will not be sufficient daylight to retrace my way back – not by a long shot. How would I find my way back in the cold and dark? I have gone deep into an ever-deepening valley and am surrounded by untamed nature.

Suddenly, a sign of hope – high above me in the rock is a monastery! It looks intact. Maybe someone's living there? Maybe they can show me the way out, or even offer overnight lodgings? The steep path I follow twists higher and higher until it reaches the gate. My hopes are kindled. I knock on the door. My blows echo in the emptiness. I spy through a gap in the timbers to the inside – the monastery is abandoned and locked up. Panic takes hold: thick clouds now cover the upper edge of the valley, I can't see the end of it anymore and it is slowly getting dark. It gets bitterly cold at night in October when you're at nearly 2,000 metres above sea level. I cry out to God. I pray Psalm 23, 'Even though I walk through the darkest valley …', and rush panic-stricken back the way I came. But where to now? The floor of the valley lies far below.

Suddenly, just a few steps from the monastery gate, I see a red arrow painted on a stone wall. It's just a little mark of paint right beside the trail. A steep path seems to lead directly into the stone wall – how did I not see it before? And, yes, there is a step, and there a stone edge to stand on …

I have to climb on all fours. With the yawning depths to my back, I climb higher and higher … but finally it's a path, finally there's hope. One rocky outcrop after another, I get closer to the foggy edge of the cliffs. I start to breathe hard. A last steep passage and suddenly, waves of relief – level ground, with a house behind it and even a road! There is such great joy in feeling level ground under your sandals! Exhausted, I drag myself the last few metres to a narrow paved road. I desperately wave at the first vehicle that comes by. It's a military Jeep and the driver lets me ride in the load bed at the back. He takes me to Bcharreh, which we reach just as night falls. I am saved.

Only when I am sitting in front of a serving of Lebanese *mezze* do I find time to reflect. The fear is still in my bones a bit, but so is the gratitude. And now the astonishment begins – the valley that is abandoned today was one of the main centres of eremitic religious life in the Eastern Church in the fourth and fifth centuries. Intercessors withdrew to this area – to these inhospitable mountain regions – to seek God in isolation. And there were hundreds of them doing this! They gave the valley the name 'Qadisha', 'the Holy'. And they sought out the most remote region that one could imagine. They literally lost themselves in God. I almost got lost myself in the wilderness of the Holy Valley.

I dip a piece of flatbread in the tahini and ask myself, where today are the people who are so lost in God that they choose a way of life like that of the ancient, now long-dead inhabitants of Qadisha? Are there people today who set off on overgrown, even dangerous paths on the great search for God?

MIXED REFLECTIONS

Two years later, and a few hours further to the west, we often took off in the early morning hours and spent the day in silent prayer and hiking in the unspoiled landscape of Athos. Again and again, we were warmly received in a *skiti* or monastery; a simple place for the night awaited us everywhere, as did a strong coffee, heavy with cardamom, after a long liturgy. And even if the pilgrim's meal occasionally consisted only of watermelon and dry bread, because it was, once again, a fasting day, the taste of this kind of life stayed with me always, deeply calling into question my own western habits.

Yes … the monasteries of the Eastern Church! I experienced much that was impressive on Athos and much that was strange. Much that was beautiful and alive, but much that was obdurate and narrow. Discussions that went on all evening, with monks who were filled with a missionary zeal and thought they sensed potential converts in us. Nights spent in prayer, fear and terror when we got stuck on the peninsula in a storm and missed our flight back home.

But the encounter with a way of life that is lost in God, in which everything is focused on God, left such a deep mark on me that it became part of my personal definition of radical Christianity.

THE FIRST LINES

We reach a monastery again. This time in late autumn. We have come on a small boat from Lerissos. That afternoon, we have followed the winding hiking trails along the coast from Esphigmenou to Vatopedi. Under us are the azure blue of the flashing sea and the majestic silence of the holy mountain. And now, after Vespers, we are standing between black Cyprus trees on the cobblestone square in front of the church, and talking with a bearded monk (which is no special marker, they all have beards here) about life in a monastery. There is no purpose to the world. There would be no purpose to any of it, if one only thinks of the earthly. He points to his thick, black prayer book. 'This here is life on earth,' he says, and opens to the first page. His fingers follow the first line: just this here. And the rest, the other lines on the first page and the other hundreds of pages – that is life in eternity. And that's what it's about. The monk is a nomad who lives for eternity. How radical is that, what he's saying? But how true.

What would a life lived truly according to these principles look like? What would my day look like if I were to live according to other laws entirely? It would be the life that was described in the Sermon on the Mount. Everything Jesus talks about in this manifesto for discipleship (Matthew 5–7) deals with a lifestyle that only makes sense in the light of eternity! What sense does it make to repay evil with good if there is no justice that goes beyond death? What sense does it make to be faithful and pure in sexuality – even down to what we look at and think about – if life is short and you're supposed to enjoy it? What point is there to wasting time praying and studying the word of God, if life is just about whether to kill or be killed? Yes, Christian life on earth is well summarized in the monk's metaphor of the first line of the book. All the splendour, but also all the suffering, of earthly life lose their significance in the light of eternity. Eternity. An ocean without a coast. Endless space without walls or floor. A time line that never ends on the right side … 10,000 years … 1,000,000,000,000 years … 10,000,000,000,000,000,000 years.

In fact, this could be the lesson of Athos: a place that lives only for eternity and reminds people of eternity and that is withdrawn from the laws of this flow of time. My visits to the holy mountain of the Orthodox world, and to those abandoned monasteries in Lebanon, awakened a longing for this eternity in me, and a longing for a place where eternity takes shape. There are already many good books on this, and many good ideas, but the question rising in me was where are the places where exactly such a life – a life that contradicts all earthly plausibility – becomes tangible? And where are the places that are more accessible to the youth culture of the twenty-first century than the cliff-guarded peninsula of Halkidiki – where we heard wolves howling at night, got lost in the underbrush in broad daylight, and prayed fearfully when the storm smashed the thin windows of the half-decayed Russian monastery we were staying in?

STOKING THE FIRE

To what extent does the thought of eternity shape the decisions you make in life? Take some time in prayer and imagine you are standing before the Judgement Throne of Jesus. This should not be a threatening scene but a realistic one. The moment will come when the entirety of our lives will be subjected to a loving, but deeply truthful and unwaveringly honest, evaluation through the eyes of Jesus. Everything that was straw, hay or clay will burn. And only what's real will remain (1 Corinthians 3:11–13). From the perspective of this moment, how do you assess the decisions you are currently making in life? What would you like to do differently? Certainly, you won't wish that you had watched more television when you stand before the Judgement Throne of Christ. You were made for eternity. What decisions do you want to make in prayer today?

THE ENDLESS ONION
Prayer and Character

LAYER AFTER LAYER

Chora Sfakion, Crete, August 2007
It will never cease to enchant me: the distinctive Mediterranean colours, the deep turquoise of the flashing sea against the explosive bright green of new pine branches. I love pine trees – nothing comes close to the smell of them, mingled with that of dark, rustling eucalyptus leaves, anywhere on the Mediterranean.

The view is breathtaking. The white cubes of the little village nestle in the arc of the bay far below me. Only now does a pleasant wind start to pick up. The long march of several hours, totally alone, through the Imbros Gorge, was exhausting. Stones and oppressive heat. Sheep. Narrow, winding cliff paths. Feelings of loneliness, for most of the time. Then suddenly the stone path opens up and crosses the hill country, towards the sea. And now, a view of the southern coast of Crete. It is here that Paul, on his last sea journey, stopped off before a storm nearly brought his pilgrimage to a fatal conclusion. The broad curve of the coast lies far below. The ice-cold stream from the water tap brings some life back into me. I sit down, all sweaty, to rest in the leafy shade outside a café. I have strong Greek coffee, and pastries with honey and feta – which are called *tiropita sfakiana* – and my small black Bible, my companion on so many journeys, is open in front of me. In the green, blue and ochre of the afternoon, time seems to stand still for an hour. Eventually I go down to the harbour.

BOMBER IN PARADISE

'Café Paradise', is written on the rough white wall of a building in blue brush strokes. It seems to have come down a bit in the world, this paradise, but there is still some charm between the fig leaves. It's so quiet here.

So beautiful and peaceful. The village seems asleep – old men under a chestnut tree, boats moored in the harbour rocking quietly back and forth. There is something nightmarish, though, when one is in such an idyllically beautiful place and then suddenly comes upon the wounds of its past: Crete was occupied by German forces in the Second World War. And this very harbour that glistens so brightly in the sun was strafed by German fighter planes. There were many casualties on the side of the Allies, and there are horrific pictures of these events in the souvenir shop down on the wharf. I ponder it: the cruelty of the human race. I think about the inexplicable fact that completely normal people can do such monstrous things in certain situations. And I wonder what God thinks about it. I ponder it as I arrive at the little bus station where a bus is supposed to pick me up in the late afternoon and take me back to the other side of the island, to my wife and children.

A few tourists with rucksacks are already waiting at the bus stop. They too have come here on foot, or by boat, and are now waiting to take the bus to the city. The last bus of the day. There is nothing but wilderness around, with just a single road leading over the mountains into this little hamlet. More hikers arrive. Young Australians with colourful backpacks. Two Frenchmen. We exchange pleasantries, asking each other where we come from and where we're going. But there are more and more of us. Anxious glances betray the fact that I am not the only one starting to wonder if we will all fit on the bus. And what if we don't all fit?

The stream of tourists does not slow down. The crowd grows to sixty, seventy, eighty. And now people begin to jockey for position. Where exactly will the bus stop? And where will the doors be? Some are beginning to push their backpacks forward discreetly in order to get a better place in line. Others position themselves alongside, rather elegantly, to be ready to jump the queue if they get a chance. A thousand thoughts race through my head. What happens if I don't get a place on the bus? I don't have a phone. Jutta and the kids will worry. I have hardly any money – where would I stay the night?

Shouldn't I try to get a better place in line, too?

In the meantime, some latecomers attempt, quite brazenly, to push forward. No one wants to miss their flight, spend the night outdoors or even just change plans. Neither do I! I am so tense I could scream. And although inwardly I rebel against the thought, I know it would not be right to push ahead in the line. It would not be right to not trust in God in this situation. It would be right to take the last place and just pray quietly …

The bus arrives. There is only one. The queueing people begin pushing, shoving, running and pressing. Those who were so nice and civilized seconds ago, turn into real bullies. The bus stops about ten metres in front of us to the right. The people in the crowd pick up their things and run. People overtake each other, push their way forward, elbow others out of the way. And I stand still, full of worry inside, but also full of certainty that I must not participate in this wrestling match. The bus comes to a stop. But suddenly the unexpected happens. The doors don't open. Instead the driver puts it in reverse. The driver turns, drives back, and the doors open – *exactly in front of me.* The crowd races back in panic while I calmly get on the bus and have my choice of seats. I look around the empty bus, amazed …

Of course the story ends well. Because soon a second bus comes along and everyone is able to get on. On the twisting, turning drive back through the barren mountain landscape I return to my thoughts from the harbour. What lurks in the hearts of men and how does God deal with it?

THE WAY OF THE ONION

That little episode in Crete taught me a lot. It taught me the thing about peeling an onion. An onion consists of many layers, and each layer can look very different! And people also have many layers. Outwardly everything can look fine. But there can be rot concealed at a deeper level. In fact, every one of us has a problem with this rot. Beneath an outwardly civilized and friendly façade, pure egotism hides lurking within each one of us. The egotism that says, 'Push *your* way forward!' The egotism that says, 'The other guy should get out of *your* way!' This fundamentally evil disposition does not come out quickly, of course. It is only in extreme situations that it becomes clearly visible. Situations of panic, fear and suffering can be like knives peeling back the layers of an onion, revealing the inner secrets.

Authentic spiritual life does not mean papering over real problems. Rather, it means God in his goodness allowing us to know more and more deeply that the real problem is not other people: it's in ourselves that we find jealousy, envy, bitterness, greed … And God brings this to light in his perfect timing. The many unavoidable shocks of life help in all this. Even if the shock of the day is just an overfull bus.

Prayer is like a time-lapse film of the rest of our lives. If I am upset, sad or jealous, I can easily conceal it in the busyness of everyday life. But in the stillness of prayer it all gradually comes to light. And then discouragement becomes a strong temptation – the discouragement of so much distraction in prayer. Indignation at one's own abhorrent thoughts, evil tendencies in our own hearts. Just when I want to really love God and people, I am suddenly confronted with so much in me that is negative. When I was praying at the bus stop, I recognized in myself a clear tendency of heart to want to fight for a place, just like all the others, to assert my will against that of my fellow travellers. The same impulse that was in them was in me too. And if the situation had not been just about getting a bus, but about escaping from war, bombing or famine – who knows what I would have been capable of ?

But despondency is not my only option. First of all, prayer confronts me – just like peeling an onion – with dimensions of my own reality that I would prefer to repress. But repressing them only strengthens their subtle power. Recognizing one's own weakness in prayer is therefore a great opportunity: the opportunity to look one's weakness – and one's susceptibility to being led astray – in the eye with humility. And also the opportunity to recognize that, ultimately, God doesn't love me because of my goodness. He already knew all about me and my weaknesses. He knows right now what rottenness is concealed in my onion. Patient endurance of our own shortcomings, and a merciful attitude towards ourselves, protect us from despair in prayer. This is, of course, not permission to treat sin lightly. We must declare war against sin and refuse any compromise with it. There will never be a ceasefire in this area, but that which changes me ultimately and permanently from the inside out is the loving acceptance of God. And this loving acceptance also stems from my ability to love myself in my own weakness, and from the knowledge that I can, and must, keep walking in discipleship. Yet it is only God touching my heart that can change me at the deepest level.

Man is like an onion. And God goes deeper and deeper, layer by layer. In prayer, God is not interested in pious theatricals; he's after our hearts. Wholly. That is why the path is so difficult, so beautiful and so rich.

TRUE TRANSFORMATION

In the long term, God's concern is not that we become a little bit more devout. He has nothing else in mind than the complete transformation of our hearts. He would like to see the fruit of the Spirit that Paul writes about in Galatians 5:22 flourish in the very core of our being. I have written a new and rather free interpretation of this passage in order to, I hope, make clearer what is meant by the dusty terms 'goodness' and 'long-suffering' or 'forbearance':

> *The fruit of the spirit, though, is:*
> *Love – spontaneous affection for more and more people,*
> *Joy – effervescent energy in simply being,*
> *Peace – inner serenity during outward stress,*
> *Long-suffering – the ability to consistently endure what is unpleasant,*
> *Kindness – an active interest in the well-being of others,*
> *Goodness – deeming the value of other people sacred in every interaction,*

Faithfulness – keeping my word even if no one sees it,
Gentleness – not having to coerce anything,
Self-control – taking my feelings seriously, but not always
obeying them.

I don't have to force the fruits of the Spirit through my own painstakingly rational decision-making process, but instead they become and more and more internalized – a fundamental part of the attitude of my heart. This is possible only through a transformation of my feelings, and for this I need other people. Because no one is less able to judge my own heart than I am; the unconscious strategies of our self-deception runs too deep. My own blind spots keep me from being able to act as my own doctor. I need others. Others whom I can tell of my own darkness without fear and who can tell me something approaching objective truth. The word that saves me is not one I can say to myself, ultimately.

This insight is the essential one behind the ancient practice of confession as it is lived out in the Catholic and (in a somewhat different way) Lutheran traditions. I bring myself to the light by disclosing my dark side to the assigned servant of the body of Christ, who is acting for the whole church. 'If we walk in the light … the blood of Jesus … purifies us' (1 John 1:7). In confession, you can experience this quite directly. Forgiveness, too (which is not granted by the priest who hears your confession, but which is granted by him on behalf of Jesus) is something I cannot bestow on myself but is something freely given to me and objectively declared over me.

But the basic principle of confession is open even to people who are unfamiliar with the sacramental form of confession. I need the feedback of my brothers and sisters who point out the rotten spots in my own onion peelings to me. And it is more than seldom that I need the advice of a spiritual director, pastor or therapist in order to even recognize the beam in my own eye. It is completely normal that onion layers come off faster when you pray. Intense spiritual community, confession and direction are important components of a prayer life that is growing more mature, that has moved beyond spiritual curiosity and is seeking a heart-level transformation.

STOKING THE FIRE

The absurd thing about our character weaknesses is that we don't see them ourselves. Or to put it another way: what I do notice in myself is usually not the problem. The problem begins with things that I simply cannot see because they are hidden in my own blind spot. The only thing that helps here is feedback from other people.

Usually people don't exactly react with sweetness and light when someone tells them what they find bad about them. But if I radiate the attitude that I will receive any criticism at all as an insult, my friends and neighbours will keep quiet about their irritation. They will nevertheless notice things about me that are simply not good. They won't talk to me about them, but instead, the best case scenario is that they'll keep their thoughts to themselves. Much more likely, however, is that they will talk to others about it.

But my question to you is this: are there people in your immediate circle who you know would actually tell you the truth? Even an unpleasant truth that would prompt you to change something? Imagine that you spend the whole day in the office and only noticed that you had a noticeable piece of broccoli between your front teeth when you got home that evening. None of your numerous social acquaintances in the course of the day bothered to tell you … not exactly a pleasant thought! But people would act the same way towards you if you gave them the message (expressly, or implicit in the atmosphere) that they did not have permission to tell you the truth openly.

An idea to practise: encourage two or three people you know to tell you really and honestly what they most notice about your behaviour. Accepting such truth is not easy. To be precise, it is a very difficult path of humility. But it is the way of transformation.

Another practical tip: in confession or in a context of pastoral care, really bring your dark side to light. You will see that the truth does set you free (John 8:32). There is no growth in prayer without truth – in all layers of your onion.

OVERWHELMED
Prayer and Fascination

STRUCK BY THE HUMILITY OF JESUS

Forest near Augsburg, Autumn 2007
Rays of yellow light stream down through leaves of many colours.
Insects are humming and the ground is dry enough for me to sit
down and open my laptop on my knees. I sit here and prepare myself.

The House of Prayer adventure has begun. Week after week
I teach our staff in a small chapel. It's not just our staff who are
showing up, but, increasingly, guests from all over the city.

And I am presenting my first series of teachings. The title is
'The Glory of Christ' and it's about Jesus. I spend most days except
Thursday preparing for my sermon on Thursday evening. Again
and again I cycle through the *Siebentischwald* – named after an
inn with seven tables ('*Sieben Tische*') – to the reading room at the
university library. And there I study and write for hours at a time.
Or sometimes at the lake, in the forest. Buried in the most beautiful
subject of all. Right now I am engaging with the pre-existence of
Christ. What did the Son of God do before he became a man? This
thought fascinates me. What must it have been like for God to enter
into the limits of a human existence? And why did he do it? What
was his plan? A short story takes shape on my laptop:

*Every day the beggar girl sits on the street corner. Her clothes
are brown at the edges, and she has no shoes on her dirty feet.
Passers-by amble past and hardly give her the dignity of a
glance. But today everything is different. Today she's forgotten
all of it.*

*It all starts in the late morning. A young beggar comes by.
She doesn't recognize him. He doesn't come from any tribe that
she knows of. As far as she is aware.*

At first somewhat shyly, then with a certain friendliness, he begins to speak with her.

'Who are you? Where do you come from? Where do you live?'

'Come and see!'

He sits down next to her in the dust of the street. He is friendly, kind and modest. His fine facial features evince a certain elegance, in spite of the poverty of his appearance. He shows her a respect and tenderness which this beggar girl has never known, accustomed to the rough life of the streets as she is. In his presence she feels loved, valued and full of purpose – as never before in her life. He speaks of another life, of wonderful places they can go together, of a great future. She can hardly believe him.

Everything about this beggar attracts the girl. Very soon, she begins to have tender feelings towards him. Now they share their lives as beggars. Day after day. But after several happy weeks of companionship something strange happens. Her friend is asleep, and the beggar girl wonders, 'Does he have the rest of the bread that was left over from yesterday, maybe?' She carefully reaches for his shoulder bag, fishing around in the baggy side pockets. But what's this? Amid her companion's scanty possessions, she finds some old photographs. Strange pictures of him. But he's dressed quite differently … He's wearing an army dress uniform. He's surrounded by generals in splendid attire, by fine ladies and gentlemen. One photo shows him in front of a castle, one shows him on horseback. Another on a stage, surrounded by a crowd paying homage to him. One shows him victorious in battle, surrounded by his cheering troops. Another shows him at a richly appointed table, laden with the choicest of delicacies.

Whilst he sleeps, the girl casts a furtive glance at her friend. His charming face is the same as the one from the pictures. But he's wearing the clothes of a beggar. Nevertheless … could it be?

Memories rise like a flood … That time when the royal army went through the little town, and the heir to the throne rode alongside the king and her gaze fell on the youthful prince for just a moment … could it be that it was this face, the one she's looking at now? She shudders in disbelief. But, yes, that's her beloved, who sits beside her day after day, begging. With whom she shares the mouldy bread, who shivers at night, just as she does, in clothing only a little less tattered than hers. He who is subjected to just the same contemptuous glances from passers-by as she. He who is assailed by the same curses as she. He, who sits next to her in the filth of the street. But what had moved the son of the king to abandon the splendour of his throne and become a beggar? Had he fallen out of favour?

Then, suddenly, a smile crosses his face in his sleep. Is he dreaming? He doesn't wake up, but in half-sleep she hears him murmur, 'Father, I went out to bring a bride back home.'

STRUCK BY THE MAJESTY OF THE LION

Years later, I am sitting in the prayer room and preparing for the teachings at our MEHR Conference in January 2013. We're expecting 3,000 attendees. For weeks I have been studying Jesus' conversation at Jacob's Well in John 4. And as so often before, I feel this all-encompassing fascination for the character of Jesus. It draws me ever deeper into prayer, every time. But today it is not the gentle humility of God becoming man. Today it is not the mercy of the one who approaches the adulteress at the water source with such kindness. My gaze remains fixed on the simple statement: 'If you knew the gift of God, and who it is that is saying to you, "Give me a drink", you would have asked him …' (John 4:10 ESV).

The question hangs over me now, with immovable weight: do *I* know with whom it is *I'm* speaking? Do I know his power? Or am I underestimating him, too? Of course he's the good friend, he's the teacher and saviour. But he's also Lord. And he is Judge. He is the Lamb, but he's also the Lion. Great awe takes hold of me. He is the Lion. I begin to shake a little inside, and then outwardly as well. I feel as if I could sense the breath of a lion on my skin, threatening and affectionate at the same time. It's as if I could gaze into his eyes that look right through me. After a few minutes I write down:

If you knew him …
If you only knew who it is who is speaking with you.
Do you know whom you're talking to?
Do you recognize who it is standing before you?
If you only knew who it is in whom you believe …
If you only knew who it is you're talking to …
Do you know who this is, whom you confess as Lord?
Do you know who you're dealing with?
He's untameable. Uncontrollable. Unpredictable.
He is not controlled by his enemies.
Even the ones who were sent to arrest him could not resist the power of his words the first time and went back with their work undone.[16]
Do you know him?
His enemies couldn't subdue him.
Those in power were so afraid of him that they had to get rid of him.
People who saw him began to weep or picked up stones out of fear.
He's the earthquake.
He was the terror of the powerful in his day.
He is the invincible.
He laughs the plans of the rulers of this Earth to scorn.
Do you know the Lamb of God who bears the sin of the world?
Do you also know the Lion of Judah, who rose victoriously on the third day?
Do you know that he is alive today?
The fire in his eyes has never gone out.
His disciples mocked the death sentences from their judges; they had seen him alive, after all.
Do you know the broken, suffering servant of God on the cross?
Do you know that he is alive and will return, wearing a crown

16 John 7:30.

and riding a white horse?
You have heard of the Lamb?
But do you know he's a Lion?
He has the heart of a lion.
He has the gaze of a lion.
John fell to the ground as if dead at one glance of his eyes of fire.[17]
He has the voice of a lion.
He has the determination of a lion.
If you knew the one you're talking to …
What do you think him capable of?
He's the untameable. The uncontrollable. The unpredictable.
He never had a house of his own, never belonged to a political party or ideological camp.
The only thing that the Scripture explicitly says he made with his hands was a whip that he used in the temple.[18]
He was not limited and not controlled, not even by his friends. Not even by his church. He is unpredictable.
He is the flood.
Do you know him? Do you know who you are talking to? With whom it is you are dealing?
He is radically happy. His first miracle was to create 600 litres of the finest wine for a party where people had already been drinking.
You don't need to make him happy. You don't need to console him. He is the radically merciful one. Searching for one who will worship in spirit and in truth, he strikes up a conversation with an adulteress.
You do not have to and you cannot earn his grace. You don't have to impress him.
You think your sin is going to stop him? You think your weakness is too great for him? He's the conqueror. The victorious Lion. His determination to love you is greater than your indifference. He is so different.

17 Revelation 1:17.
18 John 2:15.

There's a reason that he laid his hand on John's shoulder and said, 'Fear not!'
Everyone who sees him starts to shake.
Everyone who feels his pierced hand on theirs should worship him. He who loved us and redeemed us with his blood.

THE SOURCE OF MY MOTIVATION

This intensive engagement with the life of Jesus became the driving force that moved me to prayer. Our start in Augsburg was rather modest; our first prayer room was a tiny room in a tiny flat, with a view of a concrete block of flats. We began by praying for five hours a day. I prayed for the first three hours, then my wife, and then our friend Julia. Gradually others learned about our prayer and joined us. What kept me going in these months was not the prospect of anything spectacular, it was instead the intensive engagement with the life and person of Jesus. 'The fire of passion is mostly lit from the wood of knowledge' – this statement from Hans Urs von Balthasar became my new motto. I devoured books about Jesus – studied everything about him. For instance, his pre-existence: that he had everything and was God, but chose lowliness and the misery of a human life just to be with us. The radical nature of the incarnation: true God, but nursed by a human mother, crying, sweating, smiling, eating and believing just like we do; the generosity of his nature; ultimately his suffering, death and resurrection and certain return. Again and again I learned this lesson: it is not our own determination, but rather a gaze fixed on Jesus that keeps the fire of prayer burning. It's not by our own will, but a fascination, held by a figure whose eyes burn with fire. In fact, nothing motivates us quite like fascination. If I am fascinated by a hobby, a new device or a destination for a trip, then the hours pass by in a flash. I devour books, spend money, my eyes light up when I talk about it, and I can hardly wait to get up in the morning so that I can do something that has captured my heart and imagination. Everyone has felt this at some time. Every person is fascinated by something and can express their enthusiasm about it. This ability to let one's self be consumed with a flaming passion for something was built into the human race by God himself. Animals have nothing to compare with this. They do what they must to stay alive. But humans can get enthused about something just because it's fascinating, just because it's beautiful.

Whatever else may hold our attention, nothing compares to a fascination with a person. You can see this in the mere fact that advertising – on the covers of magazines and our television screens – depicts people's faces more often than not. Even inanimate objects and abstract ideas can become absolutely fascinating if we see someone attractive who seems interested and excited about them. We see this most clearly, of course, in the enchanted realm of love. When you are in love, time, money and physical effort no longer matter. Every thought is directed towards the beloved. Everything about her, or him, becomes worth pursuing; the beloved becomes our most precious treasure, the subject of our daydreams.

Lamentably, most Christians experience a fascination with all kinds of created things, but pass up on the greatest treasure that has been given them. The real Christian life is just this: fascination with a person. It was exactly this that captured the attention of the first disciples. It was exactly this that drew people to Jesus *en masse*. It was exactly this that moved all the martyrs of all time to fear not even death: a fascination with the person of Jesus.

When John talks about having seen 'his glory, the glory of the one and only' (John 1:14), then this is not a lifeless, religious turn of phrase, but instead means nothing less than an encounter with the source of all human fascination. Because the same God, who placed the capacity for fascination in humanity, became human himself. Nothing fascinates people as much as another person. And nothing is so fascinating, so captivating, so profoundly overwhelming as the person of Jesus Christ.

To know Jesus truly is to become fascinated with him. And anyone who is fascinated with Jesus wants more of him. He no longer asks the questions, 'What *must* I do' to live well, and, 'What *may I not* do?' Instead he asks what nurtures his love for Jesus and what starves it. He does not ask what is the minimum that he must give (in terms of time or money for example) to be a good Christian. He asks what more can he do to give this endless beauty even more space in his life. And no wonder: that's just how fascination works. The source of Christian life is a fascination with Jesus.

LEARNING WONDER

And it is not just the everyday Christian life that draws on this wellspring of fascination, but all of Christian thought and teaching about God. According to Aristotle, wonder is the beginning of wisdom. To regard a thing as not necessarily self-evident and to take the time to stand in awe, recognizing that you really have not yet understood it – or anything at all – that is where philosophy begins.[19] This concept from Aristotle's *The Metaphysics* could be applied to theology. The very beginning of theology is, after all, an event. And the wondering, uncomprehending contemplation of the events of salvation history, and the attempt to apprehend them rationally, is the key driving force of early theological reflection. When the first Church Councils, in their professions of faith, formulated what are, even now, the defining teachings about Jesus Christ, they were preceded by centuries of these secrets being discerned, worshipped and witnessed in blood. Wonder was the beginning of theology.

But how do we handle these teachings about Jesus today? How do we handle the teaching about the person of Jesus Christ? How do we handle, for example, the original Christian dogma that he is fully man and fully God? This statement is the foundation of the Christian statement of faith. But who still believes it, really?

Many well-meaning people, who might call themselves Christians, nevertheless, and intending no malice to anyone, agree with those who are religiously indifferent: certainly, Jesus was a great teacher – his message was all about world peace and human brotherhood. Just a tolerant good guy. A Dalai Lama of the ancient world, perhaps. The statement that Jesus really is God incarnate (and the only one of his

19 Aristotle, *The Metaphysics* (Dover Publications Inc., 2007).

kind!), and is the (only!) way, the (only!) truth and the (only!) life, sounds downright politically incorrect to the ears of many 'enlightened' Christians of the twenty-first century. In this they agree with the omnipresent mainstream religion of our society – dogmatic secularism – which rejects every claim to speak of 'objective truth and falsehood' in connection with religious attitudes as fascist-leaning indecency.

God does not intervene in the world. Because either he does not exist or he is something akin to a universal principle. And in the final analysis everyone is equally wrong, just as Lessing stated in his famous Ring Parable.[20] Asserting anything else in today's society almost feels like planting a bomb.

Apparent only from the very fringe of the church scene, a view of Jesus as just an ordinary man floods the market places of the internet. Islamic apologists, full of missionary zeal, argue eloquently in German and English how the Bible itself (and healthy common sense as well) makes it absolutely clear that there's no way Jesus could be God. In fact, the attempt to refute the assertion that Jesus is described as God-become-man is one of the central strategies of Islamic missions on Western soil. The uplifting Christmas sermons that declare the humanitarian charity of a God who reveals himself in Jesus seem like the half-baked work of sleepwalking preachers by comparison. And at the same time Jesus is supposed to be a symbol of love for our neighbours. He's the good guy from next door, one of us. Of course he is. But isn't he also ... God? Wonder is the beginning of theology. And a theologian like Paul often interrupts his own train of thought to break out in astonished praise.

Beyond all question, the mystery from which true godliness springs is great:

He appeared in the flesh,
was vindicated by the Spirit,
was seen by angels,
1 TIMOTHY 3:16

---

20 Gotthold Ephraim Lessing, *Nathan the Wise* (William P. Nimmo, 1877).

He seems literally unable to restrain it! A truly great secret. A wondrous, amazing fact he never tires of thinking about. A God who comes in human form and yet remains God. An energy like that of a thousand suns, burning in a single light bulb. And yet it does not explode. God, revealed in the flesh. A topic of never-ending astonishment for Paul.

This wonder fills all Scripture. It crowns the deep discussion about the relationship between Israel and the church in Romans 11:33–36. Before all kinds of admonitions follow in Colossians, Paul nearly seems to run out of words:

> *The Son is the image of the invisible God, the firstborn over all creation. For in him all things were created: things in heaven and on earth, visible and invisible, whether thrones or powers or rulers or authorities; all things have been created through him and for him. He is before all things, and in him all things hold together. And he is the head of the body, the church; he is the beginning and the firstborn from among the dead, so that in everything he might have the supremacy. For God was pleased to have all his fullness dwell in him, …*
> COLOSSIANS 1:15–19

And in his letter to the Ephesians we find thanksgiving, and a worshipful reflection on salvation history that reaches its apex with Jesus, filling the entire first two chapters.

IN THE BEGINNING IS AWE

Are we still able to feel a sense of awe today? Can we be awed by Jesus? If you observe the church scene in the West today, one can hardly escape the impression that the church is preoccupied with itself. What new strategy for church growth will help? How can new structures be put in place and how can the expectations of visitors be met more effectively? But what is it all really about? What is the goal, the centre and the reason behind it all? What is church really about? About itself? Is religion just a particular expression of cultural life? A set of rule-driven social rituals and performances? An uplifting collection of various values that the society would be worse off without?

Awe is the beginning of Christianity. In the beginning there was no institution. There were no rules, and not even any fixed teaching. In the beginning there was an encounter. Such a disturbing encounter that it took the new-born church centuries of rubbing its amazed eyes to truly realize what had just happened to it.

A man had appeared. He was born of a woman. He came from a certain tribe, a certain town and spoke a certain language. A man who ate, slept, sweated and could be touched. A man finally who suffered, bled and died naked on a cross.

A man who at the same time shattered the limits of all that was humanly possible. A healing or two – yes, people had seen this in the prophets or even heathen temples. But sovereign authority over all diseases, over all demons – thousands of them – authority over the wind, waves, the storm and over matter like wine and water ... Even if that could all just be explained as particularly impressive examples of God's work through an emissary, the greatest provocation and irreconcilable end of any attempt to interpret him as just an emissary is found in his words: 'But I tell you' ... (Matthew 5:22, 28, 32, 34) Jesus started this section by saying, 'You have heard that it was said to the people long ago,' (Matthew 5:21) so he's actually referring to Moses' teaching. Jesus is adding to the law that Moses gave. Who does he think he is? Who is this putting himself on the same level as God? 'Very truly I tell you, ... before Abraham was born, I am!' (John 8:58). An eternal I? A person who thinks he's beyond time? Who is this and who does he think he is, to claim he can forgive sins, when only God can do that? Even the men sent to arrest him confess, 'No one ever spoke the way this man does' (John 7:46).

What an intolerable provocation! Jesus of Nazareth existed. For centuries, all attempts to somehow find plausible alternative explanations for the rise of the Christian communities of the New Testament have failed. Jesus died. All attempts to impute to the early Christians the invention of a symbol that was equally objectionable to both Jews and pagans as their trademark leads to contradictions. But really – where is he buried, since he demonstrably lived, suffered and died? How could the grave of an enemy of the state – a grave that was guarded – suddenly be empty? And how could the message of his resurrection be preached so successfully in the city where there were eyewitnesses to his death? All attempts to impute to the first disciples the invention of such a blasphemous lie about a very obviously false Messiah fail today just as they did then, and keep in mind that most of them paid with their lives for their testimony.

And so the Christian church remains here in awe. 'Who is this? Even the wind and the waves obey him!' (Mark 4:41), asked the disciples. Who is this man who died and yet lives? And the church asked, 'Fully man and fully God – how can that be? Two natures in one entity? A human will … and a divine will, in a single person?!' Wonder was the beginning of theology.

And today? Can we learn to stand in awe again? We certainly need to. Jesus shows up in our churches. He also shows up in our lives somehow. He plays a role in our lives. Admittedly he is not the director. Jesus is part of our tradition of faith. A model, to be sure. But we rarely feel a sense of awe before him. Our gaze is not captured by him. We are so busy with ourselves … When was the last time you heard a sermon in which a fascination with and an astonishment at Jesus Christ were not just the declared intention of the preacher, but were perceptibly the heart and centre of his life and teaching?

When did you last hear two Christians talking with each other about him with this fascination and astonishment? When were you last struck with awe of him? We have forgotten how to feel awe of him. Remember: those who have met him weren't able to tear their inner gaze away from him.

And yet standing in awe would save us. By contemplating his glory, we are transformed and we become like him. At least, that's what Paul intimates in 2 Corinthians 3:18. Awe transforms, and fascinated contemplation shapes and heals the human heart. Learning that sense of awe anew, to really know Jesus and let him fascinate me: that would in fact be our salvation and our transformation.

STOKING THE FIRE

Ultimately it is not the Bible that is the word of God, but the person of Jesus Christ who is the Word of God, about whom all of the books of the Bible give witness. But often our engagement with the Bible is exhausting or raises more questions than it answers. But if Jesus is the Word of God *per se*, then the entire great story of God is ultimately about him. On the road to Emmaus, Jesus explained everything written about him in the Scriptures to the two disciples. And by that he meant the Old Testament. There is a myriad of things to discover about Jesus – even in the Old Testament!

I encourage you to read your Bible not like a telephone book or an oracle. Study the individual books of the Bible and talk about them with Jesus. Talk with him about them like you would talk to a friend sitting in a chair across from you. But don't just stay with the reading. Instead let the reading turn into a conversation. If you don't understand something, ask him to clarify it. And if you do understand something, discuss it with him. Thank him for it. Ask him to show you more of it. 'Chew' on it and contemplate the mental images that arise in your mind.

What began in the forest around Augsburg has become more and more a habit for me: reading the word of God with love. Read it like a love letter. Read it like it was written by someone who knows you, loves you, and wanted to pour out his heart to you. When I come across something I don't understand, I know that the fullness of all knowledge of God is present in the person of Jesus. I read all Scripture then as leading to Jesus who is the key to understanding Scripture.

But in a real friendship there will still be secrets. How boring would God be if I always understood everything about him? And there's a certain charm in hearing the words of Saint Augustine confirmed in prayer: '*Si enim comprehendis non est deus*' – if you understand it, it is not God. God's mysteriousness can seem strange. And it can lead to loving, sometimes silent, worship. It is the source of real fear of God and real love for him and for others.

THE GREAT MYSTERY
Pray for the Peace of Jerusalem

BORN IN ZION

Jerusalem, 15 September 2000
Suddenly, in front of me are the evening colours of Jerusalem. How many thousands before me have felt, almost physically, what the Psalmist says about Jerusalem?

> *Indeed, of Zion it will be said,*
> *'This one and that one were born in her,'*
> PSALM 87:5

When, on that day in September as I come down from the Mount of Olives for the first time, I – like so many before me – gaze at the City of David in the light of the sinking sun, and something inside me is irrevocably wounded. Once I'm back home again, my heart aches. The longing, the (home?) sickness for Jerusalem feels like a longing for Jesus himself. It is a longing that actually is that of Jesus: he longs to return to this city to rule from his throne as the heir of David.

But alongside the encounter with the external, with the sights and sounds of Israel, there was also an inner familiarity. It was learning the Hebrew language in particular that opened up a world to me that had previously felt alien and strange. The laborious training of the eye to recognize these foreign letters was like the initiation into a secret apprenticeship. An entirely different way of thinking, different concepts of time, reading in a different direction, alternative meanings of words … I learned these letters with a holy reverence; the finger of God had written them on the stone tablets given to Moses. Everyone who even learns the verb classes with which the Lord spoke to his prophets steps onto Holy Ground.

Intellectually, the little book *I and Thou*, by the Jewish philosopher

Martin Buber, challenged me immensely during this period. I read it everywhere, repeating every sentence, even while travelling. Not infrequently I would stop in my tracks because a passage had grabbed me and wouldn't let go. Buber opened up something of a personal insight into Hebrew thinking (or at least his version of it). In his view our world is essentially broken down into the basic words 'I-Thou' and 'I-It'. The way we live, speak and think is essentially shaped by whether we are in a personal I-You relationship, or an objectively-distanced I-It relationship with people, things and God. This is a relatively simple thought, which became for Buber the key to all the Holy Scriptures of Israel. This philosophical reasoning was followed by a deeper fascination for the Jewish piety movement of Hasidism (for which Buber provided an unforgettable literary monument in his wonderful *Tales of the Hasidim*).

I began to love Israel. I began to love Judaism. Far from seeing the Old Testament as only a legalistic shadow of the fulfilment in the New Testament, I fell headlong into a fascination for the Hebrew word of God. On my afternoons I even struggled through Buber's extremely idiosyncratic translation of the Old Testament in which he referred to God as 'The One Surrounded by Hosts', and the string of pearls from the Song of Songs 1:10 as 'Gleanings from Oysters'.

KABBALAT SHABBAT

My visits to the synagogues of Israel have always had a powerful effect on me, too. The word of God is loved, is prayed aloud; people dance around it, and it is preserved with sometimes fanatical zeal. The passionate, robust, enthusiastic and thoroughly masculine expression of this zeal for God palpably surrounds me on that warm evening in September 2000. The fact that I, a Christian, walk around wearing a *kippah*, with tassels under the white shirt and the *siddur* in my hand – in a way that might be misconstrued from the outside – can be put down to youthful foolishness. I will never forget the look on the face of our Palestinian host, who burst in on us as we were praying in Hebrew with our *tallit* (prayer shawls), rocking our upper bodies back and forth in characteristic Hebrew prayer posture (in the only quiet room we could find: the bathroom!). Speechless and blanched with fear, he ran out of the room.

'Are you Jewish?', he asked us later that evening over his shisha, still visibly bewildered. He was relieved to hear that we were Christians, and his remaining preconceptions about us disappeared into a puff of apple-scented tobacco smoke without further comment.

But now I am in the Jewish Quarter. I am surrounded by men. Lots of men. They are praying loudly, calling, singing, shouting. The mood is almost like that at a soccer match. And Tom and I are in the middle of it, at the table of one of the many rabbis; he is praying the '*Kabbalat Shabbat*' (the first prayer of the Sabbath on Friday evening). When one of those praying asks me what page we're currently on in the Hebrew prayer book it is a real high point for me.

I find myself at the Wailing Wall, the object of the deepest emotions in Israel and the greatest hopes for a Messianic restoration of God's people. The scanty remains are all that is left of the Second Temple. In the large open area there is a sense of happiness and zeal. The sky over Jerusalem still shimmers blue in the west while the first stars are becoming visible over the Mount of Olives. The rustic circle dance, and the almost bellowed, shouted singing of well-known songs like '*Lecha Dodi*' or '*Od Avinu Chai*', bring an uneasy reminder of how passive men can often be in our Western Christian churches and communities. How sentimentally, one-sidedly effeminate some of our prayer often seems. I dream of a place for such aggressive prayer, such a holy pugnacity, that I see (and above all, hear) from my Israeli prayer companions.

A couple of steps to our left is the start of the covered section of the Wailing Wall synagogue. There are books on every wall: commentaries, prayer books; on every table there are mountains of books. The ceiling is a semicircular brick structure, the synagogue itself a long corridor along the Wailing Wall. The noise of the courtyard is somewhat dampened here, the air a bit more humid, the voices of those praying only a murmur. In the yellow lamplight a few figures stand, most of them clad in black coats or suits. Each of them is holding a prayer book. Every eye is fixed on the ornate script of the Hebrew letters. A script that, with its points above and below the letters, constantly forces the eyes to move quickly up and down. Letters that make your eyes dance. The upper body moves in the rhythm of prayer; the lips are almost mute. Some stand so close to the wall that they could kiss it and some do exactly that with great tenderness.

Can it be true that the *Shekinah*, the manifest presence of God, went into the Western Wall after the destruction of the Temple and is most clearly perceptible in direct physical proximity? In any case, there is something deeply familiar, physical and intimate about this complete immersion in prayer over open Bibles, about the movements, and about the proximity to the wall. I dream of a Christian house of teaching like that of the Hasidim, in which the word of God is searched out day and night. I dream of a Christian synagogue like the one on the Wailing Wall, in which God's word is considered, prayed aloud and wrestled with day and night, with love and zeal. In which prayer is loud and fierce and then once again turns tender and personal.

THE LITTLE WAILING WALL

These recollections return to me one day as I take my usual place in the Prayer Room and supervise. I am standing directly in front of the wall of our small, refurbished shopfront, with its white curtains and colourful pin spotlights. We've been praying here since our group outgrew our flat. This is our first real 'House of Prayer'. God's word is open in front of me. I started my shift at 8am and I will stay here and pray for another couple of hours. Other intercessors have prayed here before me, from 4am until 8am, 2pm until 4pm, and midnight until 4am, and of course yesterday. Nearly everyone prays out of the word of God. And nearly all of them move around a bit while they do. At times some will stand directly in front of the white front wall. Others sit and study Scripture, read commentaries, write in their journals, underline passages in their Bibles. Once intercession begins the almost meditative baseline mood of the Prayer Room transforms into a militant intercession for the needs of the world and enthusiastic worship of God. Something of my dream of a Christian synagogue has already become real. Even if Augsburg still does seem like a rather pale reflection of the evening colours of Jerusalem.

'My house will be called a House of Prayer' (Mark 11:17). This is what you longed for, Jesus, for your Temple. May our little room here at least be a modest echo of this desire of your heart, King of Jerusalem and Messiah of Israel.

HATED AND LOVED

Beirut, October 1999
That love for Israel and that longing for the restoration of Jerusalem have remained, of course. But to anyone who sees Israel primarily as a modern nation, perhaps even an oppressor-state, it is incomprehensible. In fact, my own enthusiasm for all things Jewish had to go through some stages of purification. Two months of working closely with Palestinian Christians during my time in the Abbey of the Dormition in Jerusalem, and many trips to the West Bank and other countries in the Near East showed me the beautiful faces of the Arab nations, and their suffering – that undid my uncritical pro-Israel attitude. And then, in Beirut, to hear the electricity had only come on again properly some days after Israel had bombed parts of the city in a retaliatory strike – that really got to me. I had quickly come to love Beirut, that crazy, wounded, ruined, pulsing Paris of the Levant.

And yet it was also precisely those trips that left me, again and again, at a loss for words when I was confronted by the sheer scale of Arab anti-Semitism. One of the many contrasts of the Near East! Yes, I became fond of this little city. My place was in Achrafieh, the run-down, predominantly Christian part of Beirut, where I talked about God and the world late into the night with friends from France and Lebanon over a shisha. Everything emanates the crumbling splendour of what had once been Bohemian. Just a few hundred metres away lies the former 'green line', the demarcation point between two parts of the city, two cultures, two armies. The front. Whole swathes of streets are completely shot up, the wounds of tens of thousands of bullets have chewed the faces off whole buildings. At that time parts of the city were still under the control of the rebels. Taking pictures was prohibited and at one point I simply turned back, because watchful eyes and machine guns were aimed at me from every direction.

Equally unforgettable was my rather foolhardy excursion into the Bekaa Valley between Anti-Lebanon and Lebanon, which, at the time of the Lebanese civil war, was controlled by Hezbollah and was the site of both the bloodiest battles and the highest-yielding drug-producing region. Our little minibus was repeatedly stopped on the way there. They were checkpoints, but not operated by soldiers. These were operated by black-clad Hezbollah fighters, all armed to the teeth.

I eventually reach Baalbek, which is also the site of the Jihadist headquarters, and street banners commemorate terrorists who have fallen in battle. A friendly street merchant invites me to tea and congratulates me on being German. Because Hitler came from Germany, didn't he, and he did so much good. Why, he killed so many Jews, after all …!

Hatred of Israel is not just a motivator among Nazis, it is also, lamentably, an integral part of every Muslim society. I do not need to defend everything about modern Israel to be appalled and horrified by the sheer degree of anti-Semitism and the ever-present hate propaganda in the Arab world.

When I open Scripture, I read of a God who loves Israel, who courts Israel and whose plans for the eschaton are inextricably linked to Israel. And I, who love this God and his Son who took on human form as a Jew, can do no more than pray for Israel and confess with the Psalmist: 'The LORD loves the gates of Zion, more than all the other dwellings of Jacob' (Psalm 87:2).

STOKING THE FIRE

The subject of Israel – why is this even part of a book about prayer? What feelings does this chapter stir in you?

It has to do with prayer because it is linked to intercession and God's will for our world. It has to do with how we pray for contemporary politics and events. It also has to do with prayer because it is linked to the plans of God's heart. Because this is another side of prayer: deepening our understanding of the plans of God's heart and submitting our own will, our own desires to them, more and more.

Do you find the subject uncomfortable? Then talk to God about it and ask him to show you his perspective on it.

Does the subject stir your interest? Then start to ask God for greater understanding in prayer and combine your prayer with Bible study on the matter. The entire book of Romans would be a good start, but especially chapters 9–11.

One last suggestion: the Psalms directly challenge us to pray for the peace of Jerusalem (Psalm 122:6). Do you pray?

BY UNFAIR MEANS
Prayer and Answered Prayers

DOES GOD ANSWER PRAYER?

Augsburg, August 2008

I sit here. I know that God does great things. I have experienced this so many times before. Yet once again I am sitting here and praying for a situation that seems completely hopeless. And once again the questions come …

Is all this prayer ever actually heard? Does the supernatural really exist or is faith just a strategy for coping with life? Does prayer truly change the world, or does it just change the person who prays?

Yes, questions that I ask myself again and again, and questions that people constantly ask us about the House of Prayer. Is what you do really worth it? Of course the answer is anything but simple. I wish it were, because it's relatively hard to identify the direct 'impact' of prayer. For example, let's ask another question: has anything changed in Augsburg since you started round-the-clock prayer?

This can never be answered generally. Most importantly because many, many people have been praying in Augsburg, and not just for the last few years! Secondly, whilst of course good things do happen in Augsburg, one can't really say whether this is as a direct response to prayer. One also can't say what the condition of our city or nation would be if we or anyone else were to stop praying, either.

Is prayer worth it, then? Ultimately, it's an act of faith: will God keep his word? Is Jesus trustworthy?

It's a bit like a marriage.

'Do you really love me?'

'Yes!'

'And how do I know that?'

'Well, you know it because of the many little details, but ultimately I can't prove it to you. If you don't believe in the depths of your heart that I love you, you could view all of these little gestures as coincidences, pretence or favours done out of a sense of obligation. I can't prove my love. But if you believe that I love you, you will find evidence of this love everywhere.'

It's similar with the question of whether God answers prayer. Ultimately the question is whether I believe in the God to whom I pray. Naturally, it is a terrific motivator when you experience answers to prayer. But if you pray several hours a week – and for several years – it becomes somewhat difficult to feel motivation to pray if that motivation comes solely from answered prayers. We will probably never see the effect of so many prayers, or see it only much later, perhaps only in eternity … And yet there are always – as in any love relationship – the signs of his attentions: the pleasant reminders that there is much more to reality than merely what we see. Our everyday life is full of such miracles, great and small. We experience God's miraculous intervention again and again. Again and again we hear testimonies of healings, answered prayers and sudden changes in apparently hopeless situations after prayer. In this chapter I would like to recount some of these stories.

ENCOUNTERS WITH THE SUPERNATURAL

Summer 2008. We are holding our first Discipleship School in Augsburg. We have rented a holiday flat as lodgings for a few young men. On the day the rent is due we give the money (1,500 euros in cash) in a sealed envelope to one of the participants to hand over to the landlady.

A few hours later the lady calls me: she says the envelope was empty. We didn't write out a receipt when we handed it over, and so now we face the question of how to deal with this situation. The young man who was supposed to deliver the money is completely trustworthy, and we are absolutely sure that the money was in the envelope when it left us. A sealed, thick, heavy envelope with money in it! Perplexed looks. When we don't know what to do, we pray. In prayer my friend Elke gets the impression that this is an attempt by the landlady to cheat us. We continue to pray. A little while later, our weekly teaching night starts, and we almost forget the whole thing.

The next morning, I am sitting having my regular prayer time, not thinking about the money at all. I am simply at peace in the presence of Jesus. Suddenly, I have the impression that I should pray specifically, here and now, that the spirit (or mentality) of deceit and theft over this woman be shattered. This impression comes without any fanfare, but with great clarity at 9.15am. A short, but powerful prayer follows. One or two minutes later, the phone rings. I don't pick it up because I'm still praying, of course. But my wife does. And on the other end of the line is the landlady. She says that the money just 'suddenly appeared' … and the matter was resolved. We didn't know how this woman would relate the story, or what was going on inside her, but the fact is that God answers prayer. And it's a good thing that we can fight with spiritual weapons!

IN THE HANDS OF THE SYRIAN POLICE

Damascus, August 2010
The capital of Syria is a staggeringly beautiful city. Or rather it was before the war: before competing militias fired grenades, and ripped to shreds so many places whose beauty I had once marvelled at. Damascus – one of the oldest cities in the world. A visit to a Turkish bath somewhere in the maze of a small *souk* remains unforgettable: the astonished and amused glances of the locals at this westerner who dared to come here; the warm steam in the Ottoman domes; the forceful grip of the masseuse on my back; the taste of sweet black tea with nana mint as I sat in the waiting room wrapped in a white towel; the smoke of the shishas, surrounded by smiling, bearded Arab faces. And then the prayer time in the large mosque that a Muslim invited me to. The large mosque in which the head of John the Baptist is still reverenced today.

But as beautiful as Syria is, it is also full of contrasts. It would not be much fun to fall into the hands of the Syrian police; the passport checks at the border crossing into Lebanon held something of a threatening character. Was the officer ever going to return with my passport?

In Lebanon an old man broke off all contact with me when he found out I had already been to Israel several times. He had lived through their civil war and the fear of the Syrian secret police was still with him. I will never forget the icy cold, dictatorial contempt in the eyes of the Syrian soldiers I met at various borders.

In the summer of 2010 my neighbours in Augsburg go back to visit the country they fled some years before: Syria. My neighbours are Kurds. They aren't Christian, but we still have a close neighbourly relationship. And so it is only natural that we witness to them about Jesus. It doesn't take long before we begin to offer prayer for their practical needs. And it helps – in passing the test for a driver's permit, in the search for a job, and in so many other ways. And so they start to believe more and more of what I tell them about Jesus. Whenever they need a miracle, they ring our doorbell.

But on this day in August they need a huge miracle. The wife has been arrested by the Syrian police upon arrival, and they have seized her passport. She has returned to Syria for the first time to visit her dying father. Years ago, she had fled illegally, and today she is caught. The delayed revenge of the regime. As a result, she can only travel within Damascus. Week after week she waits, hoping she will get her passport back. In the end, money is what is needed. At first 500, and eventually more than 1,000 euros are paid in bribes, and still her passport remains in the custody of the police. Successive agreed return dates pass, but nothing happens.

And on this Saturday her husband, our neighbour, rings our doorbell, his eyes red and swollen from weeping. There are only two days left before the date of her return flight and his wife has sat in the police station for several whole days and nothing has happened. He may never see his wife and their two girls again, because it is impossible for him to travel back to Syria. His dark eyes fill again with tears. 'Please pray!' Yes, now only prayer will help! Despair of this kind teaches one to pray. But at first it is difficult to keep hopelessness at bay. I remind my neighbour of all the times when God has already worked miracles. We will pray and he will help, this time, once again, absolutely. He seems to feel slightly reassured.

But afterwards when Jutta and I begin to pray together, we sense the battle for faith: isn't it rather improbable that the police, after weeks of waiting, and several days after receiving all that bribe money, are going to suddenly change their minds? The Syrian police, of all people? Isn't it irresponsible to raise the poor man's hopes, to tell him that our little talk with heaven is capable of doing anything? We pray, we wrestle, we lament …

After about fifteen minutes of prayer I sense that it's now up to us to take a step of faith. We should act in faith on the premise that our prayer has been heard and answered. What a challenge! So we begin to praise God and thank him that he already has answered us and that the policeman is getting the passport right now. This act of faith costs something and yet it seems exactly right.

Two hours later, our neighbour rings the doorbell again and this time he is radiant with joy, this friendly little man with the big moustache: his wife called an hour ago. She had just come from the police station where the officer had suddenly and spontaneously gone into the adjacent room, retrieved her passport and given it to her. A few days later, the family is reunited in Augsburg.

BY UNFAIR MEANS

Congo and Augsburg, 2013
Occasions for 'subversive prayer' pile up in 2013, and one theme in particular seizes hold of me. Many people don't know it but right now there are more people in slavery in the world today than at any other time in history. Most of them are living a life of forced prostitution. We have been praying for an end to human trafficking in our city for months. On the way to the House of Prayer in the evenings, you can see women on the street: many from Bulgaria, and many in the hands of human traffickers working for the mafia. Legislation to legalize prostitution, which was passed in Germany under the alliance of the Social Democratic Party and the Greens, has turned our country (and also our city) into Europe's whorehouse. Then, all at once, there is surprising news: starting in the new year, street prostitution will

be illegal in Augsburg, thereby dealing an effective blow to human trafficking. The police enforce the law with strict controls, and 'The Augsburg Way' of dealing with prostitution becomes well regarded all over Germany. Similar initiatives are now conceivable in other cities in Germany and are openly discussed. We celebrate!

More surprises follow in the same year. In the spring a report appears in the Augsburg newspaper: there is not one single doctor left in the city limits who is willing to carry out abortions (except for those very few that are indicated for medical reasons). For the newspaper editors this is a sign of a crisis in medical care, but to us it's a victory for life in our city! We have also been praying for an end to this monstrous injustice for a long time.

And it continues. A few weeks later a new law cuts the permissible business hours for casinos. There are dozens of gambling dens fostering this addiction within the Augsburg city limits, and they are open day and night. This fact has long been a thorn in our side. The House of Prayer should be open 24/7, but these places shouldn't. And then suddenly, their uncontrolled expansion is shut down!

In the spring a team from 'Youth with a Mission' brings a report to the House of Prayer about the disastrous situation of the civil war in the Congo. With hundreds of participants on site and friends connected through our webstream, we commit to pray for a breakthrough of light in the Congo. A few days later, on 18 March 2013, the most important rebel leader, Bosco Ntaganda, surrenders himself to the UN and gives up his weapons, having been fighting for years. Nobody knows why! The rebel organization, M23, breaks up a few months later. Unbelievable! Coincidence …?

In the months leading up to Germany's parliamentary elections we pray that the Lord will bring the family-destroying propaganda of the Green Party to light. Just a few days later, a series of disclosures about that party's historical support for paedophilia begins to surface. This in turn leads to their infamous failure in the September 2013 election results. All of this is not just because we prayed in Augsburg. That conclusion would be presumptuous. And yet such coincidences keep piling up …

Actually, it is unfair to the enemy that in prayer we have been given the strongest weapon in the universe, which he cannot counter. We just have to use it.

The question of whether or not prayers are actually answered becomes superfluous at some point. In my own life I have, again and again, had to despondently ask the question why a certain person was not healed, or why a certain prayer was apparently not being answered. But the sheer number of answered prayers, some of them bordering on the unbelievable, that we have experienced over the years nearly makes the question itself superfluous. In my life to date I have experienced nearly every imaginable kind of miracle. I have received letters from married couples who, after years of hopelessly trying to conceive, suddenly conceived a child after they had been prayed for. I have received letters from people whose health situations suddenly and inexplicably improved. But the especially encouraging answers are the ones to the prayers that are almost brazen. These include the story of one of our staff members at the House of Prayer.

He had prayed to God for a car, and he had the impression that God was asking him to be more specific in stating which car he was praying for. What? Ask God for a very specific car? Wasn't that impudent? And yet didn't Jesus say that we were to pray in bold, childlike faith? So he prayed for a BMW 5 series. Believe it or not, in a few weeks this staff member, who had not told anyone about his prayer, was given a car as a gift. In fact, you guessed it: it was a BMW 5 series. A few weeks later a married couple handed my wife an envelope. Inside was a money transfer receipt for the sum of more than 10,000 euros. We just stood there stunned. But our astonishment grew when Jutta reminded me: 'Don't you remember? When Tom got the BMW you said "Honey, let's pray for 10,000 euros!"' We had just moved and needed money rather urgently. I had forgotten this prayer. God hadn't.

STOKING THE FIRE

Intercession is a fascinating aspect of prayer. The best thing about it is that God does answer prayer for real. In the next chapter I will recount some more astonishing reports of the fruits of prayer. At the same time, intercession is an art that must be learned. My recommendation is that you find a couple of like-minded people to pray with. Begin your prayer time with praise. You can sing and play music yourselves or you can play a CD and sing along with it. Or just praise God in free-form prayer by saying to him who he is and what he does (which is what praise is, by the way). Then enter into a short time of listening to prayer together (which you can also do before praise) and exchange your prayer concerns with each other. I encourage you not just to pray for the immediate personal (often familial) concerns, but to ask God specifically: 'What greater concerns would you place on my heart today, Lord?'

Then make a list of your prayer points and take about ten minutes to pray for each one. If you have the gift of tongues, you can pray quietly in tongues while someone else prays aloud in your national language. Or you can just pray through the list of concerns. I encourage you not to 'work on' a given topic for longer than ten minutes total, after which perhaps sing another praise song. And the intercessors shouldn't pray for too long at a time (at most thirty seconds). Both 'rules' help keep prayer fun. You will see: intercession takes strength, but it brings great joy. And I am quite certain you will soon see real fruits of your intercession.

COLLISION
Prayer for the Breakthrough

SEX AND DRUGS – ALL COMPLETELY NORMAL

Amsterdam, November 2010

There is power in prayer. Power to change more than a single human life. But a whole group? A whole city? A whole continent? Where is the hope that lives in prayer? Where is this power for Europe?

The canals glitter in the morning light and the houseboats rock gently in the waves. Flower boxes on the windows and beside the doors; Amsterdam is a gorgeous city. I have just taught at the Mission Base for 'Youth with a Mission'. And now we are on the way to the old city – the part of the old city around the *Oude Kerk* (Old Church), which the locals also call '*D'Huurenzuil*' ('Whores' Row'). We are conducting this experiment because we don't want to be misled. Even if I were to let Tom lead me by the hand, keeping my eyes closed as we walked through these alleys, I would be able to sense exactly where and how the spiritual atmosphere changes when we cross the bridge that leads to the red light district.

What meets the visitor's eye here is shocking, all the more so due to the apparent normality with which it is presented. It is a part of the city in which the only businesses are bordellos, coffee shops and fast food stores. A part of the city where, every weekend, thousands of tourists from all over the world come to get drugs and cheap sex. A part of the city in which hundreds of women from poor countries are forced by vicious pimps to perform a kind of slave labour that far exceeds their worst childhood nightmares.

I will never forget the expressions in the eyes of these women standing in their display windows. Empty, lonely eyes. Painted eyes that synchronize with the lascivious play of their bodies as soon as a man walks by. It's perfectly rehearsed: a mask that shouts, 'Come to me', whilst empty despair opens up behind it. A new 'john' every fifteen minutes, making up to forty a day. And 'conventional sex' is far from being the only thing on offer.

In between them are the shops where one can buy highly potent hashish, and marijuana that is nearly as strong as LSD and opium were during the hippie era. In the shop windows are little golden pipes for cocaine and digital scales for heroin. And all of it is so normal. I can now see what it was I had sensed though the Spirit. What startles me the most is that I don't sense the darkness, the threatening, the evil at once. Instead I sense vertigo, confusion, a fog in my spirit. For me, this is evil's calling card: it doesn't show itself openly, but pretends that it's normal. It inverts our values.

But there is something unbelievable here: in the middle of this red light district, right next to the former headquarters of the Church of Satan, is a little House of Prayer. When you look out of its windows, you can see the nearly-naked women standing in the display windows. Two worlds collide, again.

Amsterdam is not the worst city in Europe. But it is one in which the question hits me with full force: what power can change our continent? Europe used to be the Christian continent. What can stop the downward spiral of disbelief, the destruction of our values and our hearts? What is the hope of Europe? And once again, it is the stories that teach me how God's power can break in. Stories that have to do with prayer, of course.

I have already tasted it a bit in our first power-encounters in the youth ministry: there is power in praying. Since we started the House of Prayer, the question has returned in a manner that is more and more direct each time: how does prayer grow in power? And can you actually *see* the effect? The following stories deal with these two questions.

ENCOUNTER WITH FIRE

Tirol, February 2008
Tom comes with me again. Once again I am travelling to visit a group of young people – and I'm going to tell these young people

about Jesus. But this time it's not easy: it's a small group of teenagers, somewhere in a mountain hut in Tirol. Spaghetti with tomato sauce, table football, sleeping bags, the usual. But I am about to learn something decisive this weekend that will connect with my own power-encounter from 1999. And it will be something that will shape my image of what fruitful service in the Kingdom of God looks like forever. But I shouldn't get ahead of myself.

The first evening I tell them about my own walk with Jesus; the next morning, I tell them about this and that. I'm funny, and my teachings are full of gripping stories and examples. But, unlike most times, I don't really seem to be getting through to them. The young people? They're totally normal: two girls keep playing with their mobile phones, another giggles, their attention is patchy.

Then comes the afternoon. I talk about sex. Normally this is a topic that breaks through everyone's reserve or at least ignites some interest. But here, too, the reactions are flat; the fire doesn't seem to catch. A 'Holy Spirit Evening' is planned for later because the leader, who is still pretty young himself, wants something to happen. But with our reception so far, we don't expect much. What was *supposed* to happen? The messages I gave just didn't catch fire, we've got no band to speak of, certainly nothing I would even hope could draw people in. I feel at a genuine loss because I have to keep relearning even the most basic lessons of prayer …

It's 5.45pm and Tom and I withdraw to pray in our very rustic sleeping quarters. The 'Holy Spirit Evening' is supposed to begin at 7pm, and I have no idea how it will go. We start to pray freely. Within a few minutes I start to feel something. Without looking to my left I already know that Tom feels the same thing. It's like a very heavy blanket is coming down on top of us, as if we could feel that there was some heavy, dark fog there keeping God's light from reaching these young people. As if pushed down by a load, I kneel on my thermal mat. Soon my head is also on the floor. I struggle. Or to put it differently: *something* has seized me. I am no longer praying, I am *being* prayed. Tom, next to me, appears to feel exactly the same. He is on the floor, too, weighed down by a burden of his own.

In the Scriptures, Paul talks about experiencing birth-pains for believers (Galatians 4:19). I have heard of prayer that is like labour pain, but I hadn't experienced it before. Labour pains are not something you do, they're something that come over you. And in this moment such pain, such struggle for the souls of these young people hits me, it knocks me to the floor. It breaks out of us a sigh, a lament, a cry to God. It does not feel pleasant at all. It's like being in a fight. And yet it is the only thing we can do right now. And it doesn't stop. For over an hour it does not stop.

The clock chimes. It's actually time to stop praying and start with the programme; this would be the logical thing to do. But part of the lesson we're being taught is not to stop; I sense that it wouldn't be right to stop now. So I go to the group's leader and tell him, 'The evening's going to start a bit later because we've not achieved a breakthrough in prayer yet.' The young people are sent back to their leisure activities and I go back to our sleeping quarters. There's no other option. I hardly cross the threshold when the same burden hits me with the same intensity. It feels like a huge, threatening enemy has suddenly come into our crosshairs, and the only thing we can think of doing is to maintain constant prayer as concentrated fire on the enemy's position.

Several minutes pass. Suddenly, in an instant, as abruptly as it came, it vanishes. I realize that I have stopped praying. I notice that I have become calm. All at once a peace and a sense of ease fill the room. A glance to my left shows me that Tom has also stopped praying and is just sitting there quite serenely. With a quick exchange of conspiratorial glances, we agree at once: now we can start!

FIRE

The evening begins uneventfully. No band, no games, no stories. I speak for about ten minutes. What I speak is the pure, direct, radical Gospel. You must be born again. You want to follow Jesus, do you? Well, it will cost you everything and will be the most radical decision of your life. But it will be a decision that is worth it forever. I don't use any rhetorical flourishes or jokes. The teenagers who were tittering a while ago are now sitting there as stunned as if they had been struck by lightning. I invite everyone who wants to make this decision right here to come forward, now, in front of the watching eyes of their friends.

These aloof young people – the very same ones who had seemed incapable of being moved by anything in the earlier teachings, the ones who had been so cool and 'above it all' – it doesn't take a second, and all of them, yes *all* of them, jump out of their seats and rush forward. I lead them in a simple prayer: 'Father, I thank you that you love me and that Jesus died for me. Jesus, I repent of my evil ways, please forgive me. I want to give you my life today and accept the gift of your cross. I want to follow you. Amen.'

Before we are even done praying, some of them begin to sob heavily, and one begins to shake. Bear this in mind: this is not a charismatic setting. The opposite, in fact. These young people don't even know there is such a thing. We start to sing a simple song to the Holy Spirit, and to pray for each one individually.

It's as if our hands were charged with high-voltage electricity. When we touch the first kid, he drops to the floor as if struck by lightning. The same thing happens to the second, the third … many begin to weep loudly, to sob, to scream. Another begins to laugh and repeat, 'Thank you, Jesus!' over and over again. Holy chaos, all over again. When the local priest pops into the semi-darkened room for an unannounced visit – entering a room where young people are all lying on the floor weeping, laughing or just sitting there full of joy – I can't explain everything that's happening here, not quickly anyway. All I can think of is to make a suggestion: I ask him to make himself available for confession and pastoral care in an adjoining room. He glances around at the unusual scene one more time and then goes into the room. Tomorrow, I'll explain to him what's happening. Somehow …

But when he comes back the next day, he says, 'What that was last night, I can't really say. But what I can say is that every one of those young people came to confession, and I haven't often heard confessions like that …'. Later I find out that a girl from a Buddhist family was baptized. The evening was a great victory for the Kingdom of God and a mighty, enduring breakthrough in the lives of these young people. I have learned my lesson for good: there is a difference between declaring the Gospel with power and without power. And what makes this difference? Prayer, and prayer again.

'SH*T ... CHRISTIAN!'

Kandy, Sri Lanka 2001, Augsburg 2013 and elsewhere
There is, in fact, a spiritual reality. It is invisible to us, due to a defect in our sight rather than a defect in reality. Everything, arguably, could be a coincidence. It is, perhaps, a coincidence that while I am sitting on a train and praying, a man dressed in black sits down across from me – a man with chaos in his eyes. Is it a coincidence that he then pulls out a black book with the title *Unholy Bible* (another name for the Satanic Bible) and uses his cigarette lighter to make strange symbols above it in fire? I don't let myself be distracted, and continue to pray with confidence in my heart. A few minutes later he begins to show more and more severe signs of demonic oppression. He begins to shake and tip to the left, his appearance ever more chaotic. The train compartment is full of people but suddenly his piercing eyes focus on me. And like the hissing of a snake, he spits a sentence at me in English that I don't completely understand. Something about wanting to have my soul ... As always I am not outwardly recognizable as a Christian, but the thing inside him apparently has a problem with he who lives in me. Coincidence?

Another story: I am walking through Ulm on my way to talk to a youth group about sexuality. It's one of my favourite topics. Since Jutta and I waited until marriage to enjoy sex, I have been keenly aware of the importance of this topic, especially for young people. I walk through Ulm, praying in my heart. Two bearded men dressed as Goths, with long black coats, approach me, and I look them in the eyes amiably. With the same hissing as that which came out of the mouth of the strange man on the train, one of them turns on me as he passes and spits, 'Sh*t Christian!' Again, there was nothing external that would identify me as a Christian to him. But it shows that there is a spiritual reality! I rejoice inside. He who is in me is greater than he who is in him. And darkness fears the light.

I could tell many similar stories. For example, a story from a city that looks like it sprang out of an oriental fairy tale. The city is Kandy, the holy city in Sri Lanka. Located on a lake, the massive temple reigns over the middle of its noisy streets. It is the Temple of the Tooth. It's called that because the tooth of Gautama Buddha is revered there, and is daily honoured with a magnificent sacrifice of more than forty different curry dishes. Reverently, the women, dressed in their colourful saris, line up in the golden light of the holy hall and hand one of the saffron-robed monks a pot containing a meal, and her sacrifice of incense.

The smouldering aroma of the incense sticks accompanies us as we step out into the open air and the murmuring repetition of the half-sung verses is engulfed in the street noise of the early evening.

Here in Kandy, Jutta and I become witnesses of an unusual spectacle. Traditional dances, shaped by the Hindu belief in gods and demons, are performed. Colourful masks, acrobatic contortions, driving rhythms. The high point is a dancer, obviously in a dark trance, approaching a path full of burning coals. He walks on them barefoot. The crescendo of the drums underscores a climate of darkly fascinated expectation. Somehow I don't feel well. I sense that the atmosphere is demonically charged. But the light of Jesus is in me. The dancer steps onto the coals with his feet – apparently pain-free, but in a ghastly trance. The first steps … But then, quite suddenly, the dancer collapses. Disturbed glances in all directions. Helpers rush to his side, trying to preserve an appearance of order. The dancer doubles over, his eyes roll back and he has to be carried away. The occult spectacle is finished. Coincidence? No: there is a spiritual world. And if the light of Christ really shines within me, such a collision should come as no surprise. It is just one of many examples that only seem strange to those who don't believe in the existence of such a spiritual world.

A SPOT OF LIGHT

Again and again the intercessor is in danger of underestimating what he does. Again and again he is in danger of losing sight of the big picture. So often one does not see any immediate fruit. What does a small group of loyal intercessors, who meet weekly, really accomplish? My twenty minutes in the morning that are obscured by the distractions of everyday life – do they change anything?

Doubts can – and do – arise, even in a place that is dedicated entirely to prayer. Even here, discouragement and disappointment are real dangers. An encounter from early in 2013 shook me awake, alerting me to the greatness and significance of every loyal hour of prayer. A team of Korean Christians had spontaneously decided to visit the House of Prayer. But it was only the next morning, after they had already left, that we were even aware of them. They had left us a note that ought to fill every intercessor who has ever felt completely discouraged with renewed assurance. The note tells us their story: they had come to Germany entirely in faith and with no plan of where they were going to go. They asked God in prayer for destinations. They felt they were given a vision of a thick, dark blanket of cloud over Germany. One place caught their attention: a beam of bright light had pierced the fog and had driven away all of the shadows with its light. They did not know their way around the country, but they booked train tickets to the place that they had seen in their inner image; it was more or less in the middle of southern Germany. Once they got to Augsburg, they continued following that divine direction, like the Magi from the Orient following the star.

The story may sound like a fairy tale, but a few hours later they were standing in the foyer of our House of Prayer building and they knew, 'This is the place.' They prayed until deep in the night, and left us a short note explaining the background of their brief visit. A note that can remind even the most insignificant intercessor that he is part of a greater history and a divine strategy even if he sees so little of it.

Of course, we don't think our House of Prayer is the only spot of spiritual light in Germany. Not by a mile. We just think that God sent us these dear Korean brothers to remind us what the dignity of every Christian really is: to be light in this world of darkness. This reality is not lost on the intercessor – this reality, with its struggle, but also with the conquering power of the true light.

STOKING THE FIRE

What group, what church, what family or what place moves you personally? Where do you hope for more of God's power, an in-breaking of his light? It works best to pray with others when one is engaged in 'prayer warfare' aimed at a breakthrough.

Search for like-minded people and discuss how you perceive the spiritual atmosphere around this social group or geographic area. What shapes the mentality of the people there? What 'spiritual vibe' do you pick up there? Is the climate constraining, dark, depressing, grey? Or is God's light something that can be perceived there, and do freedom, openness, warmth, creativity and a readiness to help others reign?

But don't get stuck in the paralysis of analysis. Instead, do something about it in prayer. You do this best not just by 'praying against the Evil One', but by instead petitioning for the Good. Light does not overcome darkness in a room by actively attacking the darkness. Just turn on the light – and darkness is already defeated. This attitude should also shape our prayers when we pray for the spiritual atmosphere. We pray best with our minds focused on victory. For example, when you pray for a church, don't pray against 'envy and unreconciled conflicts', but for honest love, for reconciliation and for the Spirit of Christ.

The prayers from the New Testament Epistles can serve as our models. They are, without exception, 'positive prayers'. Take one of these prayers in your hand and pray for the group or place in question. You will see change. Not immediately, but gradually.

Prayers from the New Testament letters:
Romans 15:5–7,
Ephesians 1:15–23,
Ephesians 3:14–19,
Philippians 1:9–11,
Colossians 1:9–12,
1 Thessalonians 3:9–13,
2 Thessalonians 3:1–5.

SONG IN THE NIGHT
Prayer and the Battle of Praises

A SONG IN THE MIDDLE OF THE NIGHT

Jemaa el-Fnaa, Marrakesh, Morocco, June 2010
The shadowy realm of the night unleashes a frenzied spectacle. During the day the 'Place of the Dead' is a bright spot in the heart of Marrakesh, frequented by tourists – a broad clearing amidst the confusion of the alleys. Alleys without names, twisting, half-dark alleys that come to a sudden dead end. It is impossible not to get lost in the *souk* of Marrakesh. A collision of voices and aromas. And everywhere the colourful, dripping wool bundles of the dyers hang from the roofs. Indian yellow and the *rouge de Marrakech*, the blood-red of the carpet weavers.

But when the muezzin gives the call to evening prayer and the shops in the bazaar close, everyone seems to head to the 'Place of the Dead', the former site of public executions. The broad square in the labyrinth of alleys changes shape: hundreds of booths are set up. Orange fire shoots out of the mobile cook shops and smoke from the ovens rises above the improvised tables, covering the whole of Jemaa el-Fnaa. Those who have a liking for sheep's head and snails sit down at the stands. Others are drawn into the swarming darkness of the square by the rhythmic beat of Berber music, which some describe as one of the global strongholds of the forbidden arts and occultism. The snake charmer shoves a cobra in my direction, and the tarot card reader casts prying glances at the passers-by. The tumult on the square seems to grow ever louder, ever more frenzied the later it gets. Finally, the sun goes down and it is only the flickering fires and the light from the smoking cook shops that illuminate the spectacle of these thousands of black, rushing figures. In all the folklore on display I sense something dark that seems to be gazing through the crowd with eyes like a predatory cat. Or am I just imagining it?

Through a poorly lit side-alley, I find my way back to my shabby night lodgings where I am renting, for the sum of eight euros a night, a small room that is inescapably reminiscent of a prison cell. The dull, many-voiced hammering of desert drums lulls me into an unquiet sleep where strange shapes rush through my dreams.

The next morning as the Moroccan sun rises over me, I sit on the flat roof to have my prayer time. As I look out over the sea of tin roofs, domes and minarets, a familiar and uncomfortable feeling creeps over me. My thoughts flow slowly, and my spirit feels like it's stuck in place; the freedom I usually have in prayer is replaced by a strange sluggishness. In spite of the gleaming morning light, there is something dark over me, like a nebulous vapour that gives way reluctantly to the inner clarity I usually know in prayer. This is a lesson about what we call 'the spiritual atmosphere', and immediately I recall the moment when I first had this feeling …

DUSTY AIR

Al-Azhar University, Cairo, Egypt, January 2006
Why are the two young men forcing their way in front of me and trying to keep me from photographing what's beyond them? I want to take a picture of the most important Islamic university in the world, which is beyond that fence. The noise of car horns, the grey of the concrete buildings, and between them the picturesque masonry and calligraphy that make the mosques and the madrasas recognizable on the street front. The bustle of Cairo crashes in on all senses from all sides. Spices, taxis, plastic flowers, grilled meat, exhaust fumes, patchouli, graffiti, veils, posters of Mecca: all this makes Cairo.

I spend the night on a tour bus. Beside me sits a chatty Egyptian, who loquaciously recounts the historic victories of the glorious Egyptian army against the Zionist aggressors. He spits a lot as he talks and keeps edging closer. I'm forced to sit next to him for hours. I arrive at the bus station just before dawn, exhausted; the only people stirring are the refuse collectors. I stumble around in the endless streets of this megapolis. On the first bus I get on, there are recitations from the Koran on the loudspeakers. On the next, an action film playing on the small screens. The plot depicts heroic soldiers discovering a conspiracy – an Israeli spy is trying to poison Egyptian children. He got the poison from a Coptic priest who gave it to him in the sacristy of a church …

And now I am standing in front of the Al-Azhar Mosque, and I am still slightly puzzled as I hold a little booklet that a friendly guide gave me in the mosque: 'Women in Islam'. A pathos-laden pack of argumentation explaining why only Islam offers women true freedom, about the Christian oppression of women, and why most women thought it was just great that their husbands had other wives.

The fact is that here, even in the years before the 'Arab Spring', Islam was not showing its most amiable side. And why is everyone staring at me? Are the students bothered by my keen observation of the university from the outside? I'm praying in my heart the whole time; what's going on behind these barred windows that I gaze up at as I pray? Why do I seem to be immediately conspicuous, out of the hundreds of passers-by, so that people try to stop me from taking pictures? Why does my very presence feel like that of a person walking through a dark room, suddenly caught by the beam of a flashlight? If there were such a thing as spiritual odour, then something would stink here. I've experienced it before, about a year ago …

A LESSON AMONG THE SHARDS

Bonn, August 2005
We meet to pray at night and sing in the trams. We are attending World Youth Day 2005 with a group of friends. The newly-elected Pope Benedict XVI has come. We walk past a fast-food kiosk, and out of the train station into the open air. A newspaper stand … a bakery … My eyes pass over a haggard figure whose empty eyes seem to be searching for something on the ground. She drags herself over to a small group; they all look broken, somehow. My friends and I decide to explore the green parkland next to the train station for a

while, and we quickly recognize that this is not an ordinary place. Somehow, there is something foul about it. Men sit on the park benches and drink schnapps. An older lady with red hair, and only one canine tooth, puffs away on a cigarette – her clothing is worn out. There are two young prostitutes and some punks. We see a man who is skeletally thin, his wrinkled skin covered in tattoos – even his face. There are expressions on faces which have been hollowed out by years of drug abuse, there are shards of glass on the ground.

The year is 2005 – the wild year when my friends and I try to see just how insane we can be for God. It is the year of our 'Face your Fears' events, of entire nights spent in prayer, and the first steps towards establishing the House of Prayer. And so, we decide that we will witness to Jesus in this dark place: we spread out in teams of two to talk to people and offer to pray for them. But this turns out to be a bit harder than we expected.

At least the young girl with the pink hair and the piercings listens to what we have to say, but the bald, gay prostitute with his leather jacket wants nothing to do with us. The alcoholics laugh, others curse us … things don't go quite right, but still we continue; we really want to share something of God's love with these people. Finally, we approach a figure sitting doubled over on the ground, wearing a thick jacket. Her knees drawn up, her head bent down, she turns out to be a young, thin girl. There's a rolled-up sleeping bag next to her. She does not react to our greeting. We approach slowly and ask if we may pray for her. We nudge her. When she doesn't respond to any of this, we gently lay hands on her shoulders and begin to pray. Then the older red-haired woman with the missing teeth approaches us and asks us in a raspy, alcohol-slurred voice, what we're doing. 'What, you're praying?' Now we notice that the skin on the girl's wrists under her sleeves is full of puncture marks. 'Yeah, it's good to pray for her,' the older woman says, 'She's seventeen, and seven months pregnant.'

For a moment time seems to stand still. She's seventeen, hooked on heroin and pregnant. Somehow, I manage to say an 'Amen' and bring the prayer to a conclusion. We creep away as if someone has beaten us about our heads with a club. Our attempt to bring light to the 'Pit of Bonn' (in German the *Bonner Loch* is what people call this area around the train station) was a rather miserable failure. What an embarrassing attempt – we have face-planted on hostile ground. We came in like trespassers without any authority. It all feels so dark, so discouraging, so hopeless. Yes, the spiritual world is real, and this place is as dark as night. Somehow the spiritual feeling is similar to that in Cairo or Marrakesh ...

Despondent, we trudge back to our lodgings. I never want to go back there. Not me – no way. But not everyone in the group sees things that way: it is entirely due to the persuasive powers of my friends that I eventually let myself be convinced to brave a second attempt the next day. But this time it's going to be different, for me at least: there is no way that I am going to talk to anyone. The only thing I'm willing to do is play worship songs. That's it. And that's what happens. A dozen young people and I make our way back into the 'Pit of Bonn'.

We set up in the middle of the park and start singing. I play guitar. Contemptuous laughter starts with the first chords. I can feel the eyes of the mocking junkies on my back. There must be hundreds who meet here every day to look for drugs, sex and a little money. We stand around in a circle. Cobblestones and glass shards. I don't pray for the whole of the first song. I close my eyes and my only concern is trying not to feel the looks of those around us. The atmosphere is oppressive. Dark. I want to leave. But I keep playing.

On the second song it gets easier. 'Be exalted, O Lord!', we sing. And I begin to muster a little faith. By the third song I've made progress: the atmosphere is largely blocked out, and our attention is focused more on God's greatness than on the misery of the conditions. And now the laughter has stopped. Our hearts grow lighter and the praise flows. We sing about the light of Jesus that shatters the darkness, but suddenly the voices don't sound so harmonious.

OK – who's singing off-key? I open my eyes. It's two homeless guys, beer bottles in hand, who have joined us and apparently want to sing along. And diagonally across from us, someone else approaches: it's the spent-looking woman with the dyed red hair and the bad dentition. She tries to join in, too.

I close my eyes again. Now there is a sense of freedom and joy, the surroundings are forgotten, and I am completely immersed in worship. The next time I open my eyes, it is because I suddenly only hear my own voice singing. What has happened to everyone else? Surprisingly, I see that they are all involved in conversations with the people who have joined our circle, coming from all directions and wanting to participate. It doesn't take long before we pray together, and the first tears begin to flow.

In the end, I put down my guitar, because once one junkie has heard that his friend was prayed for, he wants it, too. The prostitutes and alcoholics pray with us, opening their hearts to Jesus their saviour and redeemer. A man talks to me. His whole body, his entire face, the skin on his head and even his eyelids are tattooed. He looks like a reptile. Then he tells me about his abusive father, how he became homosexual, how he started hustling. We listen, we tell people about Jesus, we pray and see how God's love flows into their hearts. Since we don't have any tracts with us (we did not anticipate this happening) some of us give away our Bibles. Tears, laughter, prayer and singing fill the whole square. And hours later, when we finally leave, people wave us off like friends who they hope will come to visit again, soon. The whole atmosphere of the place has changed – it now radiates light.

LEVELLED PATHS

Again and again I have experienced it: praise levels a path for the light of the knowledge of God. One can quickly learn to discern that there are places and situations in which darkness appears to rule (like I sensed in Marrakesh and Cairo). But what can penetrate the darkness?

To be able to answer this question, one has to keep in mind how darkness comes into being: it is not because of the absence of God or that his power is insufficient. He exists and is always good and always sovereign. However, in his goodness, he made himself and his action, in part, dependent on whether we believe in him or not.

And to 'believe', I have come to understand, has a lot to do with the focus and direction of one's gaze.

What am I allowing to impress me the most: darkness or light? In my first visit to the 'Pit of Bonn', my attention was entirely absorbed by evil and darkness. That's why the darkness seemed to get bigger and bigger. On our second visit, though, we let praise level our path.

What is praise? Praise is the conscious act of turning one's inward gaze to God and making his beauty and greatness more important to you than all the darkness and sorrows you face. This is not always easy, of course. Nevertheless, it is a matter of proven experience: those who look only at the visible can only act according to the visible. Those who turn their eyes to God in faith experience how his presence breaks in and changes the atmosphere.

Perhaps the most impressive example of this principle from the Bible is a story from Paul's first missionary journey. He and his companion, Silas, are arrested and beaten with rods. They are then locked in prison and their feet put in stocks. How would we be feeling if an evangelistic outreach were to end like that? We read of the unbelievable in Acts 16:25; Paul and Silas not only didn't sleep that night, they sang praise songs! One can hardly imagine the scene: their untreated, bloody wounds lie open on the filthy straw, their feet are painfully bound, the filth and vermin of a primitive Roman prison …

But praise fills this place! And suddenly the miracle happens: the fetters spring open, the prison guard rushes in and ultimately even has himself baptized that very night.

But the pivotal moment is exactly when Paul and Silas start with their praise; they don't wait until after the miracle. The decision to praise God comes at a time when the visible testifies only to failure, pain and darkness. Praise, in spite of all of these problems. They are more impressed by God than by all the darkness that they see. And suddenly his power breaks in. That's what praise is all about, and that is what prayer is all about. There is always a good reason to let yourself be discouraged by your circumstances. But when we praise God in the midst of every circumstance, a way is made for these very circumstances to be changed. And even there, where we cannot see it yet, we want to be the ones who don't wait to start praising God until dawn breaks in every part of our lives; we will start to sing our songs now, in the middle of the night.

STOKING THE FIRE

Praise means saying (or singing) who God is. Make an alphabetical list and search for a characteristic of God for each letter. Or more than one. For example: Approachable, Better (than I think), Charming, Decisive, Energetic, Friendly, Generous …

If nothing else comes to mind, open up the Psalms and let them inspire you (they are also wonderful to sing or pray as praise). Once your list is finished, pray through it – thank God for what he is. Praise means looking away from one's self and one's own concerns and looking up to God. Exactly this act of directing one's gaze is what you practise if you consciously say who God is for a long time. You will see: your own problems will gradually become less important and your awareness of God's sovereignty will increase. And it is exactly this that releases his supernatural power in our lives – and changes the spiritual atmosphere around us.

WASTE
Day and Night Prayer

NARD, ONE HUNDRED PER CENT

Bethany, maybe 3 April, AD *29*

It is the first hot day of spring. The wind turned in the night and is now blowing warm air from the Negev over Bethany. The last week before the great feast; a few dozen pilgrims have already arrived and are seeking accommodation in the small village right behind the Mount of Olives, just as they do every year. Busy traffic on the streets, the bleating of sheep, the shouts of children.

The last days have been difficult. Hiking through the villages, arguments with increasingly hostile Pharisees and rabbis, whispered assertions of a murder plot … In all of Jerusalem, people are talking about Jesus and the resurrected Lazarus, and disturbing rumours are coming from Herod's palace.

Even Jesus is exhausted; the route from Ephraim was dusty and steep. They started in the morning and are now looking forward to their reunion with their friends in Bethany. Jesus has been somewhat strange at times in these last few days. He spoke sorrowfully of their pilgrimage to Jerusalem, of conflict, of treachery and dying. How good that this is forgotten for the time being, as they see the little clay huts of Bethany that hang so close to the edge of the hill, the synagogue with its blocky roof beams, the village well. And here, as everywhere, are children running around, villagers who stare curiously or wave joyfully. Jesus is back – and once again, everyone knows it. But he doesn't preach today, doesn't go to the synagogue and doesn't perform any healing.

A small, cobbled road leads to a stone wall; it is a few steps from the centre of the village to Simon's stately home. The widowed spice merchant who contracted leprosy a few years ago was cast out of the village, and died soon after. Now it's the house of Lazarus and his two older sisters, who take care of him and the household in place of his parents.

'Schalom lach, Marjam', Jesus greets her as he enters the house. Full of joy, Mary turns around, 'Jeschua! Schalom lecha!', she cries excitedly. 'I didn't know that you were all going to come so early! Have a seat!' Now the disciples come in, too. Martha and Lazarus rush in. 'It's great that you're all here!', says Martha and passes around a clay bowl with water for hand washing. 'You must all be hungry!'

Martha immediately disappears into the kitchen. Lazarus reclines at the table.

'It's so good to be back here!', says Jesus and takes a sip of water from the cup in front of him. Oil lamps are lit, bread and a spiced dip passed around.

Jesus is the guest of honour, the friend of the family. 'Tell us, Jesus, where were you all? One hears that you allegedly have some enemies?' The disciples recount the journeys of recent weeks, the miracles, the arguments …

Then Martha returns. 'You have to taste this wine! I bought it just for Passover, but I want to give you this bottle today!' Pickled olives, sheep's cheese, raisins and fresh, crispy flatbreads: a feast for Jesus. Salt is passed around, herbs and olive oil in a small bowl for the cheese. Pleasant conversation ensues – shared memories, happy occurrences – and repeatedly a word from Jesus that causes everyone to take notice.

All at once Mary rises from the table. She's been quiet until now – as always, she looks only at Jesus, listening intently to his words. The table talk, the food, the work – all that seems to happen in the background. She disappears into the side room and her absence is hardly noticed for a few minutes. When she quietly returns to the living quarters not one of the guests notices. In the shadows, outside of the light of the oil lamps she approaches Jesus. What happens next, no one saw coming. It takes a few seconds before anyone can react to it: under her arm, Mary is carrying a skilfully made alabaster amphora, shimmering in warm rosé tones. It is one of those flasks that one sees at the markets among the spice merchants – only they are usually smaller. The flask is sealed. It is immediately clear to Martha and Lazarus what Mary is doing here. They know this flask.

Their father Simon had inherited a small shop from his father. He purchased mastic, labdanum and other resins used in incense from Persian traders in Jericho and resold them in Jerusalem. And he expanded the business: fine spiced wines from Lebanon, red make-up from Tyre, cassia from India and cloves from Egypt. The perfumes and mixtures for embalming he produced himself and added to them from a small collection of the finest and most expensive aromatic oils.

Being able to acquire such a quantity of nard oil at once was a rarity, but it was the deal of a lifetime: pure, high-grade nard from the land between the Euphrates and the Tigris. He only got a few drops to smell as a sample, but that was enough: this was the finest nard oil he'd ever encountered. Before his eyes he saw the dozens of large amphorae of balsam mixtures, to which he could give a magnificent aroma with just a few drops of this aromatic essence in each. The price of the oil was high. He had to pay a large portion of all the money he had. 150 … 200 … 250 … 300 silver pieces he counts out on the caravan leader's table. But with this scent he will be able to create high-value perfumes for years and make a good return.

All of this shoots through the minds of Martha and Lazarus: their father died two years ago; as the oldest Martha had inherited the house, and Lazarus the money and the field on the hill. And Mary inherited the still-sealed amphora. The nard oil is Mary's whole inheritance – her financial security, her dowry, and with it her only chance to find a husband, have children and a secure station in society.

It is exactly this alabaster flask that Mary holds in her hands and … with a decisive action she breaks the neck of the flask and begins pouring the contents over Jesus' head. Eyes widen, and jaws drop in shock – she *pours* the oil out completely. That oil, a few carefully measured drops of which would be sufficient to lend a king's bedroom a paradisiacal aroma.

But she doesn't stop. A thin, glistening trickle springs out of the broken alabaster. It wets Jesus' thick hair, runs down over his forehead, and saturates the hem of his garment. Now she reaches down to Jesus' feet. She pours the oil out generously over them, too, massaging the perfume into them with her hands. Like an explosion of graceful redolence, the flowery essence takes over the whole room. Sweet, oriental, seductive and endlessly penetrant, awakening a thousand associations and enthralling the senses. 'What is she doing?' Incredulity is written on the faces of all the guests. But that is not nearly enough. With a quick motion, Mary takes the veil from her temples and undoes the wooden hairpin from her thick, dark brown hair that now cascades down in long ringlets. With her head now very near Jesus' feet she twists her hair around them like a towel and begins to dry them off.

That's definitely going too far. Everything is soaked in nard oil: it's dripping from Jesus' head, his clothing, his feet, Mary's hair, and flows down on to the fur blanket on which Jesus is reclining.

'What is she doing?' Judas explodes. 'That's nard oil! It's worth a fortune! You could have sold it for 300 denarii and given the money to the poor! What a senseless waste!' The others join in: 'That was her inheritance!'

'If only Simon knew!' 'That's really going too far!' 'Why doesn't Jesus say something?' 'Just imagine – 300 denarii!'

But Jesus appears not to notice this. Quiet, and more knowingly than smiling, he looks at Mary whose eyes are unflinchingly locked on his.

'Leave her be!', he says, as if he were talking more to her than to those around her.

'You will always have the poor, but you will not always have me. I tell you, wherever the Good News is proclaimed, people will tell the story of what she did for me here.'

A few days pass. His hair and garments have not been washed since. It's the day before Passover. Mary's nard is still in his thick, curly hair when the first blow from the club hits his head. His forehead seems to still shimmer with that oil when the thorns, long as your fingers, rip through the skin of his head right down to his skull. When they tear the clothes from his shattered body, his garments still smell of the spiced oil, as promised in Psalm 45. When his feet are pierced with nails, they still bear the remembrance of her hair on his skin. And in the last moment, before Jesus loses consciousness on the cross, he smells nard oil on his own skin.

She did what she could. She poured perfume on my body beforehand to prepare for my burial. Truly I tell you, wherever the gospel is preached throughout the world, what she has done will also be told, in memory of her.
MARK 14:8–9

DAY AND NIGHT?

Again and again I am asked why we in the House of Prayer think it is so important that prayer be non-stop, 24 hours a day. Does God really care whether we cover certain hours or not? Then there's the more general question: 'Isn't it enough that every Christian prays personally at some point during the day? What is the purpose of this emphasis on praying around the clock?'

Admittedly, only a few are called to choose a lifestyle that is dedicated to 24-hour prayer; I think that only a very small group of people really has this assignment. This does not mean that it is insignificant. Indeed, only a few are called to go into the mission field in foreign countries, only a few are called to become Christian politicians. And yet we need all of them. While it is quite common in our country to show a lot of sympathy for the necessity of Christian social services, schools or communities, the apparently one-sided emphasis on prayer often finds a poor reception, even among believers. And yet, I think, Christianity would lose something vital if it were not for those who make prayer the centre of their lives. That is one of the lessons I learned in the monasteries. From the very start, these people were like the second lung of the church: if the church only breathes through her proclamation – service to the poor and good social projects – then something in her dies. What dies? Ultimately, love. Because the expression of love always ends in extravagance. I learned that from Mary of Bethany.

Visitors to the House of Prayer are always surprised: twenty-two staff members, expensive furniture, power and heat – day and night – just so a couple of people can pray? And *only pray?* Couldn't these young teachers, graphic designers and academics really accomplish something meaningful in the world? And should they not work for the poor instead of singing songs to God all night long that nobody hears except them? Isn't that all a spectacular waste of time? And money? And skills?

These are understandable questions. Questions that are asked again and again. Our answer is always: 'Yup, it's a waste. Prayer is always an extravagant waste. But it is necessary. Love never shies away from extravagance. Love never shies away from extravagant abandon. Praying means learning to love. And every expression of loving extravagance toward Jesus is infinitely worthwhile to him.' 'She has done a beautiful thing *to me.* ... wherever this gospel is preached throughout the world, what she has done will also be told, in memory of her.' (Matthew 26:10–13).

YOU ARE WORTHY

Philadelphia Airport, May 2011
I am sitting on the floor and weeping. All I really wanted to do was to use the two-hour layover in the airport to read my Bible; I had found myself a remote gate, nobody but me. In front of me there is a window, and beyond it parked aircraft are being refuelled. The sky is a radiant blue. All I want to do is just read my Bible. But then I hear a song in my headphones – a single simple line of a praise song. 'You are worthy of night and day worship, you are worthy of unceasing adoration.' And all at once, with full force, something comes over me that I had sensed already in many hours at the House of Prayer yet had never found the right words for: yes, he is worthy to be worshipped day and night.

This airport is in operation day and night. So, too, are fire stations, A&E departments in hospitals, even McDonald's. None of that surprises us. No one is shocked by this, because there are clear values behind these institutions that make such pursuits seem justified. Because we know the value of a human life, we are not offended that doctors and nurses work nights to save the lives of the sick. Of course, they must! And because we value our homes, we want fires to be put out if they occur in the middle of the night. The fire department is ready for action day and night – of course! But this apparently goes even further. The double cheeseburger could, in an unexpected emergency, save you from starving to death in the middle of the night; this is why the McDonald's drive-through should never, ever close!! Because satisfied appetites and consumption for its own sake are prized values in our society, at least from the way we act.

In fact, the lights are on 24/7 for those things whose underlying value we recognize. But what is of the greatest value of all? The key? There is a fixed point – the centre of all value in the cosmos, its gravitational centre. The value of everything is determined relative to the value of other entities and creatures; gold is valuable because it is rare and is significant to human beings. But the ultimate and highest value in the universe is not even the inestimable value of a human life, but the value of him through whom, and for whom and for whose honour it was created.

God is the immovable centre, the massive reality compared to which everything else is just a shadow, fleeting and unstable. His value, his dignity and his glory are the highest and most significant values in the universe. Glorifying him is the most urgent necessity there is.

And just as it is a fundamental injustice if the value of a person is disregarded and ignored, it is a gross disorder and insult to the dignity of God if he is not praised as he deserves. Because he is worthy of the highest praise, of total veneration. It is inconceivable that a professional fireman would spontaneously cancel his night shift just because he has found something else to do that night. But it's equally wrong for people (and God's people at that!) to give themselves over so completely to the 'cares of the world and the deceitfulness of riches' (Matthew 13:22 ESV) that they completely forget what is really necessary (Luke 10:42).

THE FIRE SHALL NEVER GO OUT

Augsburg, June 2011, 6.02am
When I return from Philadelphia, I am in the grip of the reality of how completely worthy of our praise God truly is. Every hour in which people in my city are working, watching TV, studying, but in which there is no place where *HE* is constantly exalted causes me pain. I wake up in the morning with the almost overwhelming realization: God must be praised! My wife and I are actively getting up earlier and earlier, rearranging our daily schedules so that she can be in the prayer room early while I take care of the children. And then come the delightful hours in which I get to do what I have, until now, only dimly and insufficiently recognized as my life's vocation: worship God.

It does not take long before more and more of our intercessory missionaries at the House of Prayer begin to have experiences similar to mine. I receive many emails like this one: 'Johannes, could I be in the prayer room thirty hours a week instead of just twenty?' And more and more intercessors arrange things so that they can be there at night, or at 6am. So much so that we sometimes have a parking problem in the bike box in front of the little shop that we've converted into a prayer room.

In tears I tell our staff how the Lord has ignited my heart for prayer that never stops. Others tell of encounters, dreams and impressions that they have received and which all point in the same direction. It only takes two months before our entire staff unanimously decide that we are going to start with 24-hour prayer, introduce a six-day 'prayer week' and come to pray even on bank holidays. Suddenly missionaries arrive who begin a night shift every day (midnight until 4am, 2am until 6am, or 4am until 8am: six days a week!), volunteers who help with the weekends … and in September 2011 we finally get there: all 168 hours of the week are covered by intercessors. Since then the fire on the altar has not gone out.

The results that follow are amazing. More and more staff are added, more and more visitors and fellow intercessors join us. Thousands of, predominantly young, people flock to our annual

MEHR Conference, and in 2012 we are able to move into a building of our very own. It's a large centre, and through spontaneous, unsolicited donations we are able to pay for the building in cash. Debt-free. That's a testimony all to itself. And since then, this former fitness centre has turned into a furnace of unceasing prayer, nourished by one basic truth: God is worthy of praise.

ONLY ONE

Augsburg House of Prayer, 23 November 2011, 10.08am
'I want to see what the angels see, I want see what the elders see,' sings one of our singers (in German, of course) in one of the many spontaneous refrains that regularly arise in our prayer times. See what the angels see?

Our whole life in the House of Prayer, all of our spiritual energy and intensity, is driven by a fundamental conviction and experience: whoever has experienced something of God can do nothing other than love him. And often our love falters, or fails, when we don't. We have too little knowledge of God. If we knew more about him, we would be more passionate in prayer. If we were to take more time for him, abandoned worship and joyful praise would be the logical consequence.

An extremely arresting Biblical depiction of this principle can be seen in the throne room scene in Revelation 4. John the Evangelist, the seer, is given a vision of that holy place where God sits enthroned. The focus of this chapter is remarkable. It does not describe the heavenly dwelling places, the different classes of angels (or whatever other aspects of heaven your imagination might expect), but the seer's entire attention is focused on the centre of the scene: 'At once I was in the Spirit, and there before me was a throne in heaven with someone sitting on it.' (Revelation 4:2). Indeed, it is not just John's attention that is focused on this point. Everything seen, everything that is happening, is arranged around this centre point. All eyes are fixed on him, the one on the throne. He is the compass point to which everything else refers.

And how do these creatures who stand from eternity to eternity in his presence react? What does seeing God constantly do to them? Do they tremble before his majesty and silently await his orders? Do they work or bring sacrifices to earn his favour? Do they contemplate him?

We read that they do something else: they do not rest day or night. They never fall silent. Ceaselessly, every moment, they cry out, 'Holy, Holy, Holy!'. They stand in amazement, expressing their reverence in constant, unending worship. No breaks, no holiday – consumed by this service and enthralled by the magnificence of the one who sits upon the throne.

But why do they do that? What is the secret of this constant, voluntary abandon to the worship of God? We discover it when we take a close look at the description of the four creatures who worship before the throne of God. The description reads that they are covered in eyes, all around (Revelation 4:8). This depiction, which seems bizarre at first, should not mislead us into not taking them seriously, simply because we can't visualize what they look like; why does John mention that these creatures have so many eyes?

Everything in heaven – as on earth – was created by God. And God created every being so that it is optimally adapted to its environment. A fish has fins because it lives in water. A polar bear has thick fur because it lives in the northern polar regions. And what do creatures who live directly in front of the face of God need? Do they mainly need hands to do more work for him? Do they need giant brains to think more expansively? Do they need feet to run off on divine errands? None of these 'necessities' exist in the face of a holy, completely sovereign God!

What do they need, then? They need eyes. And a whole lot of them. Before a God who is like jasper and carnelian, who is compared to the most beautiful things that an author in Greco-Roman antiquity could imagine (see also Revelation 4:3), from whose throne thunder and lightning come forth, who is surrounded by a rainbow. In short, who is breathtaking, overwhelming, magnificent. Before him, creation has one job: to gaze on him and be filled with awe.

The fruit and the result of their gazing at God is obvious.

'Day and night they never cease to say, "Holy, holy, holy, is the Lord God Almighty, who was and is and is to come."' (Revelation 4:8 ESV).

They cannot stop worshipping. And they do this voluntarily. There is no mention anywhere of some little angel who stands guard and makes sure that no one stops worshipping (or administers little electric shocks when one of them misses a 'Holy!'). These creatures praise God because that is the most normal reaction in the world, when one sees God.

If we were to see him more, to know him better, then our lives will look different, will change. But the reverse is also true. If we want to love him more, then we must get to know him better. If we want to follow Jesus more closely, the first step is to get to know him better and every experience with him, no matter how small, brings a little knowledge and this generates hunger for more of him. This flows back into joyful, constant worship. Day and night.

David prays:

> One thing I ask from the LORD,
> this only do I seek:
> that I may dwell in the house of the LORD
> all the days of my life,
> to gaze on the beauty of the LORD
> and to seek him in his temple.
> PSALM 27:4

and his prayer echoes in our hearts. Yes, Lord, I want to see you. I want to contemplate you. I want to be awed by you, fascinated with you. Is that not the beginning, the origin, the generator of Christian life? And even if our sight and our experience on this side of eternity will always be 'in part' (1 Corinthians 13:9), this still applies: 'Ask, and it will be given to you' (Luke 11:9). Blessed be the hungry. Lord, I want to hunger for more of you. Truly: 'Let me see what the angels see', so that I love you and worship you as you deserve.

Back in Bethany: yes, Jesus is sitting in the midst of disciples and theologians. They all like him as a teacher, as someone to talk to, as their rabbi. But there is only one person in the whole scene who seems to know and see who it is they're dealing with here. It's the one who is not afraid of extravagance, but who pours out her most precious possession on his feet. What a waste? It's no waste at all for the one who loves. There is no such thing as waste, born of love for Jesus, to the one who sees just a bit farther and knows who and what he is. We can learn that from Mary of Bethany.

STOKING THE FIRE

Have you ever 'wasted' anything for Jesus? Or is your spiritual life more characterized by checking the minimum requirements, maybe a 'necessary evil', even? In every relationship, something extraordinary happens when we go beyond that which is 'absolutely necessary'. Of course, she doesn't need an extra serving of ice cream, but getting it sure makes a difference to my daughter. Of course, it's not 'necessary' for me to give my wife flowers, but what would our relationship be without these little acts of extravagance? It is precisely the same in our relationship with Jesus. With respect to him, our most valuable resource is usually time. And that's exactly where to start. Waste some time for Jesus! That sounds a bit threatening at first, because we all have far too little time. But an extravagance born out of love is only that when it costs us something.

My tip: plan a whole or half day given wholly to God sometime in the next six months (maybe even in the next couple of weeks). Plan it like a necessary visit to the doctor or attending a friend's wedding. Regardless of how you arrange this day, select a period of time that really 'costs' you something. You will see: it won't be without consequence for your heart. And Jesus is worth it.

ONE BRIDE
Prayer and Ecumenism

A STRANGE ENCOUNTER

Jerusalem, September 2000

Blistering, buzzing midday heat. Sabbath-quiet in the stone-white
new district. What an honour it is to have been invited to lunch
by the rabbi himself, to the second feast of the weekly holiday.
Certainly, the many questions I asked the owner of the religious
bookstore in the Old City and my evident eagerness to learn about
Judaism helped; he reached for the phone then and there, and soon
it was clear that we should meet at the rabbi's house a few days later.
And he's one of those rabbis who makes no bones about his zeal
to convert non-Jews. The meal (countless cold dishes, in countless
bowls, set on little plastic tables placed all over the living room),
the songs, the explications of Torah given in English: it's all very
impressive. The hospitality with which a foreigner, a non-Jew, is
received here is touching. But even more memorable and confusing
is the encounter on the way to the rabbi's terraced house.

We get out of the city bus, which is nearly empty, at some stop
with a name like *Zalman Shragai* or *Bar Ilan*. I look out over a
crisp, white, newly-built district with no idea where I am: silent
intersections in the blazing midday heat of Jerusalem. We ask a taxi
driver where the street is, the one with the rabbi's house. 'Oh, you
want to see the rabbi!' Our local guide, who is about sixty, amiably
gives us some directions.

He goes a few steps with us, chatting gregariously. 'Yes, yes it's
really something with those rabbis. Everybody has a different one.
There are so many groups among the Jews, aren't there?'

We're dressed in black and white, and I have a *siddur* under my
arm (I don't remember whether I was wearing a *kippa* or not). He
apparently thinks we're Jews.

What he says next remains to this day a statement about Christian unity, the utter audacity of which exceeds everything that I have ever heard before or since: while the Jews have so many different denominations, it's totally different among the Christians (of which he was one). There are no divisions, only Christians who are unified in their belief in Jesus. Isn't that wonderful?

The complete assurance with which our Arab companion presents this outrageous statement immediately leaves me speechless. We thank him profusely for his help and go on our way. A few minutes later, we are received and hosted warmly without any questions about our religious convictions. A man freshly converted to Judaism (and already attired in a proper black suit and black hat) is greeted as a guest of honour – a heavy, sweaty man with a luxurious beard. He's from Amsterdam. The honour due to a heathen who has joined the House of Israel exceeds that of any Jew, explains the rabbi, to the applause of his students.

To this day I don't know whether I should reject the statement of our Christian taxi driver for the bluntness with which it completely inverts the facts or admire it for the naïvety with which it somehow expresses a profound truth. Yes, on a certain level he is completely right! In fact, all disciples of Jesus are part of a single family. And yet a couple of years later, on a trip to Belfast, I had to witness, painfully, how far removed from visible reality his little infelicitous attempt to recruit for Christianity really was.

In autumn 2009 I had the privilege of speaking about the House of Prayer at a European meeting of Charismatic communities. The meeting was held in Assisi, and there were intercessors gathered from around the world. Invitations to visit the widest variety of countries came out of these encounters. I was astonished: suddenly, there were groups, churches and abbeys in many nations that had a longing for more prayer, who were wanting to learn everything they could about the House of Prayer. Since then I have been witness to an amazing development across the world; groups are rising up whose key hearts' desire is that prayer never stops, twenty-four hours a day. One astonishing characteristic of many of these initiatives is a heart for Christian unity. In Latvia, Italy, Hungary,

Romania, Lithuania, Poland, Croatia, Holland, the Czech Republic, Belgium, Sweden, the USA, Austria and Switzerland, I have got to know prayer movements that are all characterized by the longing to come before God together with other Christian denominations. I no longer see it as a coincidence: when you pray, what Jesus prayed for becomes important to you. And this was his prayer request the night before he died: 'that all of them may be one' (John 17:21). If God increasingly calls his church back to prayer, it will also be a call that we pray in unity: in a unity that does not trivialize differences, rather one that respects differences whilst meeting in that which unites us all.

BELFAST MONA LISA

Belfast, Ireland, July 2011
'Yes, people were killed in nearly every one of these pubs.' Rob picked us up from the train station at Newry and is now driving us through the narrow alleys of Warrenpoint. The Republic of Ireland begins right on the edge of Carlingford Lough; this is the area that inspired the landscape of C.S. Lewis' Narnia. This area near the border is where every county can tell the stories of its fallen heroes. The gentle hills and heather seem to be dreaming, before suddenly dropping off into the bay where seagulls plunge down in the water. Once again, I see the screaming contrast between the overwhelming beauty of the landscape and the tragedy of human history in it …

A few days later the black taxi rumbles over the cobblestones of a side-street off the Shankill Road. Here, in the Protestant part of Belfast, people tell their own version of the coexistence of Christian confessions. I see a playground with a gigantic painting on the wall depicting Oliver Cromwell. It's a visual depiction of him defending the faith, having defeated the Papists and avenged the massacre of innocent Protestants and the destruction of their churches. He is remembered in Catholic historiography as the Butcher of Catholics, whose actions are reminiscent of modern acts of genocide. But here he's a hero.

Clothes lines stretch across the grey backyards. Children chase a ball. And there's a painting on the side of every house. One shows a young man with the nickname 'Topgun'; a black machine gun and the date of his murder are given under his image. It occupies the whole wall. A few houses on, to the right, is the infamous 'Belfast Mona Lisa': a masked fighter who aims the barrel of his rifle directly at the observer. The message is clear: we'll hit you everywhere, on target. The image is as tall as the house it is painted on, and in front of it there are children playing … like little puppets in front of a giant backdrop.

The Berlin Wall divided the residents of the Communist East from those of the West for decades. It fell under the assault of praying, singing masses. But the wall in Belfast is still standing. About ten metres high, it separates the Protestant quarter from the Catholic. When we get to the other side we see an appalling sight: even the front gardens of the houses bordering the wall have wire barriers stretched over them. Stones or incendiaries thrown over the wall have caused damage often enough. And it's 2011 ….

Every street here has its martyrs, their heroes fallen in the fight for Ireland and Catholicism … and their terrorists. The ones people talk about in the pub, about how many Protestants they killed. Then, at the end of the story, a pint of Guinness is raised to toast the peace between religions. Admittedly, religion wasn't really the point in this battle, either for the IRA or its enemies. And, admittedly, the tensions are not nearly so fraught as they were back then when U2 sang 'Sunday, Bloody Sunday' and 'Where the Streets Have No Name' (a song referring to the side-streets in the Catholic quarter, where the signs had been removed in order to prevent the British soldiers from finding their way around). But the wounds are still open, deep and constantly bleeding anew in a climate of mistrust and hate.

The cruelty of the war in Northern Ireland leaves one at a loss. How can people holding to the same confession, that they appeal to the name of Jesus, fight each other with such relentless hate?

FROM ANCIENT WELLS

Years before this, Jutta and I climbed the Croagh Patrick – the mountain from which the legendary St. Patrick drove the snakes out of Ireland. The legends surrounding this spiritual powerhouse, this preacher from the sixth century, fill whole books. In fact, the history of the early Irish church is one of the most mysterious chapters of Christian history. We read of the conversion of an entire civilization, a culture that did not give up what made it distinctive but apparently dovetailed it seamlessly into the reign of a new High King, Jesus. A civilization whose culture was largely preserved in the monasteries and led to the impressive heights of the *Book of Kells*, an unparalleled masterpiece of early medieval manuscript illumination.

The stories of all the founding fathers of the ancient monasteries are gripping in their strangeness. We hear of holy men who sought such isolated, storm-wracked cliffs for their hermitages that their first companions died of hunger and exposure. We read of a radical dedication to God that almost hopelessly eclipses that of Christians in the twenty-first century, a radicality that became the pattern for monastic life for centuries and which lead those very monks to set off on their missionary journeys to continental Europe. Their fame endures: in the early twelfth century, Bernard of Clairvaux gave the funeral address for the Irish saint, Malachy, who had been Abbot of the far-famed abbey of Bangor, the same Bangor where, in previous centuries, the monks prayed in alternating choirs so that the praise of God did not fall silent day or night.

The famous Bangor, head of the great abbeys of the sixth century; a few thousand monks lived there. The question of how all these monasteries got started in Ireland is mysterious enough. Were there now-lost links to the hermits in the Egyptian and Syrian desert? How else can one explain the astonishing parallels in liturgy and rules of monastic life? And then there's this startling realization: continuous prayer, day and night, had already started in some local Irish abbeys in the sixth century.

We also visited Bangor; it was raining when we looked for the few remains of the legendary, repeatedly destroyed and currently abandoned abbey. This little place where, it is said, monks prayed without ceasing for more than 200 years, is just a few miles outside of Belfast. Long before Christianity split into the two major camps, and then split again and again, praise of the Lord resounded here day and night. *The Antiphonary of Bangor*, the song book for the church's praying through the Psalms, became known in all of Europe. One could even call it a real praise and worship movement that seized all Europe. And all of that is just a half-hour from the site of the street fights, the burning cars, the bombings. Coincidence, or divine reminder? How else can unity among Christians come about than through a return 'from Belfast to Bangor'? Where, if not in praying together, can fraternal reconciliation begin? Again, anyone who really prays will find that what is important to Jesus will become important to him. Anyone who really prays will pray for that for which Jesus prays. In the night before his death Jesus asks the father for unity among his disciples. He's still praying for that today. May his prayer be echoed in ours, day and night. The question of Christian unity is too serious, its history too blood-drenched, to leave it to those who simply debate it at conference tables. Only in praying together will we find the power to overcome the divisions in our hearts. The barred shop windows in Belfast and the ruins of Bangor that weep in the rain tell of this.

STOKING THE FIRE

How do you relate to Christians of other denominations? Are there certain churches you just can't relate to? Why is that? You don't have to agree with the doctrinal positions or practices of other Christians; there will always be differences at this level. But can you try to pray for a part of the body of Christ with which you have particularly strong differences? One you may even secretly hold in contempt? Jesus is monogamous, and he has only one bride. Although her visible unity is broken, all who believe in Jesus belong to this bride. Loving the bridegroom should be accompanied by an ever-increasing respect for the bride whom he only chose once. Joint prayer – perhaps with Christians from other denominations – is a wonderful area for practising exactly this attitude of heart; it allows you to be with those who are different, whilst accepting them on a deep level.

ABUNDANT LIFE
Prayer and Being

RESTING IN BEING?

La Londe-les-Maures, Provence, August 2012

Mornings are holy. A solemn dignity surrounds the first minutes of the day when you steal silently out of the house before dawn. Salt and lavender are in the air. The sea is a deep black, the sky the colour of aubergines. I trail through the cool sand, treading softly, trying not to disturb the sanctity of this hour – the hour at which the day has not yet lost any of the legendary enchantment that seems to lie in every beginning, in which one is reminded of the first day of Creation and one's cheeks redden as if shamed by fleeting thoughts of lost innocence.

My way through the fading night leads me on narrow footpaths, along bare cliffs and through thorny underbrush. Prayer seeks solitude, and in the morning, I flee the activity of the house (always full of life) and pass the first hours in the sun on a rock spur above the sea. These have been busy weeks: the birth of our daughter, Pauline, the purchase of a new property for the House of Prayer, moving, lots of visitors … eventful times. These have been eventful years, really.

And then this thought enters my life: a philosophical thought. The mere thought of 'being', and the plain statement from classical metaphysics that being is 'good' – yes, that all being is ultimately good. I don't know who is going to find such a thought rational, but in these quiet morning hours, above a sea named for its azure colour, it makes ripples like a stone falling into a still pond.

What is my being? What is being that does not proceed from having and doing? What is my being when I am presently doing precisely nothing, if there is no project and no person filling my life with activity? What is my being when nothing special is happening just now? Even when I am not thinking particularly great thoughts? What's left of my being then? And – can I rest in this state? Or must I flee it? Flee into activity, pleasure, diversion or just my own thoughts?

It strikes me with considerable force: I can barely rest in simply being, really being here, being here and being completely in the moment. The further I delve into myself and allow myself to 'listen to being itself', the more strongly I feel it. 'Peaceful rest in being? Are you kidding?!' An intimate, abundant existential moment just between God and me? That's not what I see. Sure, I pray. I pray every day. And yet it is as if there are layers that have never yet been reached by this prayer: layers of emotion, the unconscious, my ever-present fundamental attitude. There's an irritation, a sense of being driven, a sorrow, a loneliness … all of which testify to the fact that I have not completely arrived in God's truly good *being*.

Day after day, morning after morning, I return to my little secret place on the cliffs above the Côte d'Azur. A deep, unsettling awareness forms within me, unleashing a deep process that is not yet wholly finished. And it teaches me of the greatness and beauty of something I have already seen many times, but only now have the words for. And a new way begins.

OLIVES AND SAINT NICHOLAS

The Monastery of Saint Panteleimon, Athos, August 2003
His eyes are as deep as the abyss. They sweep around animatedly and then, in the next moment, radiate a serene presence. It's as though he takes the peace that he radiates with him, so that it is communicated to everyone who talks to him. Ioannikes is an elderly monk. The reverence with which the younger monks treat him attests to his special position in the abbey, or his aura of holiness. What strikes us, though, is his gentleness.

With unassuming friendliness, this bent little figure in the black cassock sat next to us on the bench under the black cypress trees in the church courtyard. His radiant blue eyes shone with keen interest from under bushy grey eyebrows and the black skull cap of his order. We were four young men, on Mount Athos once again. We had come by a challenging route, not entirely without danger. We had climbed up to hermitages on vertiginous rock walls, and spent nights listening to the mysterious sounds of the liturgy in darkened churches. These liturgies always, always included the Jesus prayer that has become so dear to us: the simple repetition of the name of Jesus that was begun by those legendary early fathers of monasticism in the deserts of Palestine and Syria in the fourth century. The Jesus prayer that is the life's breath and pulse of Athos. I hear the young monk who is sweeping the hot courtyard and withdrawing shyly from the eyes of the visitors, repeating endlessly in Greek, 'Lord Jesus Christ, Son of God, have mercy on me, a sinner.' The heavy-set Greek in monk's cassock, his face reminding one of a bearded pirate, lets the knots of his black *komboskini* (the Greek Orthodox cord for the Jesus prayer) slide through his fingers on the boat. And now Ioannikes is telling us of his prayer life. Of getting up at 1.30am, having a coffee and then reciting the Jesus prayer until 3am, making the sign of the cross each time he finishes it, and performing the great *proskynesis* with every tenth knot. This means that he throws himself completely to the ground every ten knots, that is, several times a minute. Then comes the liturgy in the church; it lasts approximately four hours. Only afterwards comes breakfast, with sheep's cheese and large, black olives.

The peace that this old monk radiates is unforgettable. His whole presence speaks of a rich life through which he has loved and suffered. And the time that he gave us! He explained exhaustively the meaning of this icon and that. He told us stories from the life of this saint and that (giving special attention to St Nicholas) and promised to give us even more extensive instruction the next day. It was 10.30pm when Ioannikes, who was well over seventy, left us, and we knew how early he was going to get up ...

BREAD AND WATER

The quality that Ioannikes radiated was one I sensed in so many places on Athos; now I call it the abundant life. A life that has everything, even though it does not seem to have much. The hornets buzz in the stillness of the midday heat, and there is donkey manure on the remote southern end of the monk's republic, which today still bears a name recalling the harsh Egyptian Desert where the first Christian monks withdrew: *Thebes*. There are no cars here – the sound of a bell on a donkey is what announces traffic. Thick maquis shrubs threaten to grow right over the narrow footpath at many points. Human civilization has not yet become the unchallenged ruler here – nature's sovereign territory self-confidently confronts that of the pilgrim. There is no music except the songs of the liturgy, and nothing that might distract. It is as if life has been distilled to its very essence, as if one were drinking of 'being' itself, purified of all scum. A potent dose of the real, with everything that is superfluous filtered out. This absence of so much that seems normal to us seems strange to the visitor at first. But already, after a few hours he will have grown accustomed to the darker bread and the more sustaining water of this life. The real shock comes when he gets off the ferry again in Ouranopolis and is hit full force by the carnival that is our Western world: advertising everywhere you look, loud noise, hectic activity and consumption. But why this overheated frenzy? And to what end?

I encountered it again and again on Athos, this abundant life. The abundant life of one who is truly poor and yet has everything. The abundant life of an old monk who has spent his years with nothing but the means to serve God, to pray and to be good to people. The abundant life that gives itself so freely, in the juicy figs along the roadside which we pilgrims often ate; in bags full of big, fleshy tomatoes – far too many! – which Father Zellerar gave us as provisions (there were four of us and the road was long); in the quiet contentment of a day in a Greek monastery, interrupted only by the striking of the tonewood and the murmur of the nearby sea; in sleep on a simple field bed next to a petroleum lamp; in the gleaming morning and noon, framed by the hours in the dark church and the ancient secrets; in the clouds of incense and many candles; in the honey-yellow white wine in the cold metal goblet (served on Sundays at breakfast with roast fish) and the mocha on one of the sagging balconies of a monastery already far too old.

STRIP CLUBS AND HEALINGS

A suburb of Kansas City, April 2007
The abundant life. What does one need to be happy? I feel so blessed, so rich, so happy that I can share in the happiness of these people. Of course, at first, I have no idea what awaits me. I had never really spent much time in areas where hard drugs are the basis of the economy. I also don't feel great when the young man, who is quite obviously on crack, rejects John's offer with a shake of the head: no, he's not coming along to the house church today. He has to go to a 'safe house'. I have no idea what he means by this, but it sounds dubious. Here in the trailer park, there are car tyres and piles of rubbish everywhere. We go back to the black van, and I ask myself exactly what I had got myself into when I agreed to accompany Matthew and John to their house church. My first encounter with Matthew was quite spectacular. 'Do you love Jesus?' was his first question. And when I said yes, he shook my hand and said that we would certainly make a good team. He's a mailman. He is also an intercessor and a messenger of God for his whole neighbourhood. And he talks about Jesus. Actually, Jesus is the *only* thing he talks about. With everyone. My mouth remained agape when he described his everyday life to me, of the female friend of his wife who was currently living with them. She didn't believe in anything, except maybe Buddha. Then, one night, Matthew came back from evening prayer with his children and she was lying on the sofa complaining she was suffering from pain. 'Be healed in Jesus name!', is all Matthew said, and her pain disappeared. That night she fell peacefully asleep to the sound of the wooden wind chimes on the door. She slept through the night for the first time in years.

The only problem was that there were no wind chimes in Matthew's house that she could have heard. But there was a peace that rocked her to sleep. She had not known peace since her abortion. And now she is pouring her whole being into getting to know Jesus.

Week after week, John and Matthew went into Kansas City's most broken ghettos and talked to people about Jesus. Then they founded little house churches. And we are on our way to one now.

We meet at Tanja's house. The house is in a run-down block of flats in a run-down area. Everything is grey. None of the doors have names on them. Children run around in the dirty hallways. No one here seems to have a job. We sit on the floor in Tanja's flat. There isn't much furniture here. The tap water in the plastic cups tastes of chlorine. Her two screaming children are with us. Tanja is maybe twenty-two, quite good-looking with a slightly Hispanic look, and tattoos in many places. Early in the conversation she tells us what she has experienced with Jesus in the last week. She had a prophetic dream for a neighbour, then prayed for someone who was then healed and talked to her sister about Jesus. She is just so thankful. Especially that she no longer has to work in strip clubs since she started following Jesus; that had not been good.

And then there is Jimmi. Jimmi looks like he has just stepped out of a hip-hop video: tattoos everywhere, baseball cap, his pants hanging down to his knees. Jimmi was on crack and his face still shows noticeable traces of the drug. He lives with Tanja. I can hardly understand him when he talks, but he does say that he is thinking of moving out. Jimmi gave his life to Jesus, too, not long ago, and somehow he senses that it's not okay to live with Tanja since they aren't married yet. Then there is Natalja, an older woman who chain smokes but wants to stop. She also tells of what Jesus has done for her, how her fits of rage have lessened. And then the topic moves to forgiveness. 'Yes, forgiveness is not easy,' says Tanja. She could sing you a song about it; she found she could only do it with Jesus' help. 'Thank you, Jesus.' Because it had not been easy to forgive her father. It was him who had given her her first fix of heroin when she was fourteen. They sit around and talk happily …

I, on the other hand, sit there stunned, listening, my mouth open, as each person tells what he or she has experienced with God this week.

And then they talk about the future. Jimmi has turned himself into the police and now he has to go to jail. He had sensed that he ought to turn himself in. What crime had he committed? The better question would be, 'What crime didn't he commit?' He had already been convicted on a charge of illegal possession of a weapon. He had fled the scene of an automobile accident and then had opened fire on someone with a seventy-two-round weapon. The police caught him and found a crack pipe in his car. He also had a fake licence. He took off again ... But now he wants to go to prison and make a clean slate of life.

We pray for him and assure him that he will not be alone in prison. Jesus will be with him. He will have everything he needs there. When the time comes to leave, Tanja and Jimmi tell me that I am always welcome to stay with them if I'm in the area. I'm not in this area often, but I leave this house with the absolute certainty that I have experienced something of the Gospel and the reality of God here, just as I have many times in the past, in prayer. In the midst of such poverty and all the broken pieces – I find *the abundant life*, one more time.

PRAYER AND THE ABUNDANT LIFE

Ioannikes, Jimmi and my morning hours on L'Argentière beach – what connects all of this? And what does it have to do with prayer?

The longer I pray, the more everything seems to boil down to a few basic questions: What is life? What makes up my life? Is my life something that happens *out there somewhere*? This thought is a real danger in prayer. In your heart you are sitting on burning coals, because there is still a lot to do 'in real life'. And then you use your prayer time to think about and plan what you still have to do. Or you encounter a deep-seated sorrow in prayer, a melancholy concerning what used to be and is no more, or what has been denied one in life – an undefined longing for a life that somehow never comes, a fear of a tomorrow that is so uncertain, an irritation with a self that isn't who one wants to be. The desire to see change in your own health, your spouse, your children, your job, the weather, because *then* ... *then* it would be, *then* I'd have, *then* I could, then ...

Yes, what, then? What would it be, your life? A fundamental question facing all of humankind, one that no one can permanently avoid in prayer, is this: is my life already happening or is it a forever-deferred future, or a past enshrouded with nostalgic longing? And does my life rest in me or is it something that is constantly kept from my reach? That others have that I don't? That I have to earn for myself? That I have to think myself into, or psych myself into? All that has little to do with the word that struck me so, that time on the beach: rest in being. It also has little to do with Jesus' promise of 'life ... abundantly' (John 10:10 ESV) and with a good Father who lets his sun rise over the just and the sinners (Matthew 5:45). In all of Jesus' words and his person is a complete trust in his Father. Such serene sovereignty lives in him. And such a real, free, expansive human BEING.

Life is abundant. It is the good gift of a good God. In him is real zest. It's already here. Now. If you really pray you learn the art of awe all over again, the joy in the zest of being, gratitude for the good of existence itself even in the simple and the mundane. I could see it in Ioannikes. He had little and yet everything. And Tanja and Jimmi had it, too: they had practically nothing and yet they had an abundant life in the middle of chaos.

Bernard of Clairvaux said, 'Things taste as they really are to a wise man'. What a revolutionary sentence! It is deepest truth. But prayer teaches exactly that: the awareness of, and joy in, what the good God created. Prayer is nothing other than a lifestyle of gratitude in which I voluntarily respond to the gift of my Creator. Ultimately everything is a gift: every minute of my life and every molecule of oxygen that I breathe was made by God. None of it ever could have been created by a human being. Resting in this being, accepting it and gratefully affirming it, is true abundance. The abundant life. And this is what prayer consists of.

STOKING THE FIRE

Gratitude and silence seem to me to be the most important aids on the way to a life in the abundance of being. Do you cultivate gratitude? Unfortunately, it does not grow spontaneously. Take time and write down a hundred things for which you could be grateful. You will see, it will take a while but really it is not difficult to find a hundred things.

Do you cultivate silence? It does not grow spontaneously either. But without silence, life becomes flat and the colours dull. Silence teaches me to bear with myself. Silence teaches me the precious value of each moment. Silence makes me open and sensitive to that which is given to me in the here and now. For the encounter with a person. For the inconspicuous, the beautiful on the roadside of the everyday. And for God's wonderful, concealed presence in the midst of totally normal life.

BEAUTY
Prayer as Art

PHTHALO BLUE AND CARAMELIZED CHILLI

Metten, Germany, Thailand and New York over the years
A lush red cascades out of the brush and drops in a thick stream onto the canvas. Suddenly, the endless white depths have a provocative centre. A ragged line emerges from the point of the broad graphite pencil, sweeping across the surface of the picture and splitting the white space into two halves. What is the relationship between the line and the red spot of colour? A picture takes shape, a secret is created, a world comes into being inside the world …

It has never been difficult for me to see the parallels between the intercessor and the artist. Whenever I've had the chance to watch artists at work – and I've had many chances – I've learned something about prayer. One was Mr. Rauch; this old art teacher had eyes that constantly darted about, and I only got to know him near the end of his life. I had started painting; seduced by our first visits to museums, I had discovered my father's box of watercolours. Eventually I got my own brushes, unleashing the enchanted realm of gouaches, and tubes of paint that bore mysterious names like 'phthalo blue', 'deep madder' and 'cadmium orange'.

The old artist had said that he was prepared to give this young man private lessons. There seemed to be something sacred about his studio: the smell of fresh oil paint; the afternoon light falling in through the large window at an angle; the quiet; the Indian yellow and the earthy brown tones still partly liquid on the wooden palette; the half-finished picture on the easel, the canvas still half-virgin; and his alert, old child-eyes, constantly observing, constantly amazed. From him I learned composition, the internal consistency of a picture. He painted almost exclusively in an abstract style; it was all about shape, the integrity and accuracy of a line. We dealt with colour only as a marginal issue. He wanted to teach me something different: the symphony of form and the inner law of materials. Charcoal is different from pencil, watercolour totally unlike acrylic. Paper, wood, stone.

Art was more than just a hobby to him. He had painted, designed and taught art his whole life long. And in my case, he taught me to see more, most of all. The structure of leaves, the form of crystals, the pattern in blossom. His art was steeped in reverence for the Creator. It is the hubris of man to want only to create something new, but it is the greatness and the dignity of the artist under God – guided by the masterpiece of nature – to bring one's own work into the realm of the visible.

His searching scrutiny of my pictures was unforgettable, as was the depth and seriousness of his assessments. Was the colour of this particular surface right, or not? Did the picture adequately embody the tension between the static and the dynamic, between profundity and conciseness in form?

The important thing to him in all this was not the effect on an audience; it was art itself for whose sake it was important that the artist develop his talent to the utmost.

I observed the same thing in artists who work with language. My first teacher was Albert von Schirnding, an aesthete in the classical sense. The castle he lived in was filled to the rooftops with books. He was an ardent lover of Antiquity, publisher of several Greek works and a great admirer of Wagner and Thomas Mann. And he was a poet. I sent him my first poems, and from him I learned to wrestle with the concision and purity of the word itself; the syllables of a poem that always say more than they surrender at first glance. More, perhaps, than the poet himself suspects. The poem: a vault into which one can descend, floor after floor, until the light of reason is swallowed by the unfathomable …

And even in a finished poem, the effect itself is not the point. Does everyone understand it? Couldn't one say it more simply? To me, these are foolish questions, showing a misunderstanding of art. The poem should itself cry out for perfection in its linguistic architecture. The poet is its servant: the poet-artist, as immortalized by Rainer Maria Rilke in his 'Letters to a Young Poet'.

I have even encountered art on my plate! That may seem odd, but I have never forgotten the first morsels of a truly royal menu that was served in Hua Hin, Thailand. What beautiful thing in white was floating in that aromatic broth? A bright green note of chilli cut through the creamy sweetness of the coconut. A seductive perfume of oriental flower blossom in contrast to roasted fish … was it galangal? The bitter-fresh orange of turmeric root … bold composition of the most contrasting flavours! This somewhat bizarre juxtaposition of flavours, almost jarring, shooting through the entire range of possible tastes, is something I have encountered again and again in Asian cuisine. Days followed in the markets of Bangkok and the small towns of Laos like a visual demonstration in the prop room of a strange sort of theatre: the sticky rice wrapped in banana leaves, the oranges and kiwis spread out on bast mats, the green heaps of pak choi and kaffir lime leaves.

Only later, on tasting experimental dishes made by a New York chef, who combined Asian and European ingredients as though creating an expressionist collage, did I begin to understand how much art was hidden in cooking. The gently-warmed fish with the essence of Thai basil and caramelized chilli. All the ingredients and even the accompanying wine made one concentrate completely on the taste of the halibut; they contrasted with it but did not dominate. Highly crafted precision at every point, a perfect arrangement of colour. This surrender to a product of nature, the human reverence before its uniqueness, which must be preserved. Human imagination, too, through colour and form, through taste and flavour, through texture and sequence to create something new and unique.

Yes, cooking can be an art form and a form of composing. Just like playing piano, as I began to understand during endless hours of Bach's Fugues and Chopin's Nocturnes. The highest abandon to an ideal of beauty, reverence before the great work and the readiness of the interpreter to give one's self over to the work: the art in music, as my strict piano teacher, and many others, taught me in so many, so different places.

What a weird thing, art! And from many individual encounters I began to develop an idea of how much it has to do with true prayer.

BEAUTY FOR ITS OWN SAKE

You can't understand art. You can't take possession of it; it takes possession of you. And anyone who is overwhelmed by it, remains bound forever. Once you've been struck by the beam of its beauty, you will carry it with you forever.

Something that especially struck me in the course of my learning has been abstract art. Only there, where the image itself has become the message and does not get its significance from its 'statement', does art seem to become that which it is actually supposed to be: *l'art pour l'art*. A work of art that exists for its own sake. It follows its own rules and demands that the artist completely enter into its service.

Prayer is an art form – a highly demanding art form. Part of what makes art art, is that it is a massive waste of time. Art that can be endlessly beautiful, but endlessly demanding, challenging. Art that exists for its own sake and finds its real fulfilment when it is no longer subject to any 'why?'. Art that is not instrumentalized. Art that is a play between the Creator and the creature in whom he planted the longing for unlimited beauty, cultivated for its own sake.

What would a nation, a culture, a city be without art? There would be hospitals, streets, factories and city halls. But all of it would suffocate in deadening functionality. The life-giving breath of simple beauty would be nowhere to be found. This horrific image mirrors the lives of many people (and even some Christian churches!). Pure functionalism is the death of what is truly human.

He who prays begins to withdraw from the dictatorship of immediate utility. He serves someone else. He does something that at first glance makes no sense, and whose ultimate value can never be calculated, one-for-one, on a scale of efficiency. An intercessor gives witness to the objective value of a God whose significance far exceeds anything earthly, as the artist gives witness to the objective value of the beautiful and the true, which demands to be expressed in the earthly.

Admittedly every art must be practised; the German word for art, *Kunst*, derives from the word *können*, meaning 'skill', 'ability'. Far too often we think that we are able to do something just because we know about it. But if art came from knowledge, we would call it 'art-i-fice', and not 'art'. (A Carmelite monk told me that joke.) Yes, prayer has something to do with practice. 'Teach us to pray,' the disciples ask Jesus (Luke 11:1), and Jesus seems to find the question superbly rational. Are we ready to practise prayer like an art? And are our churches and Christian groups schools of prayer, where one finds masters of this art, as one can find them in many different artistic disciplines? Can we show others the way?

Art is, ultimately, deeply fulfilling. The question of what art contributes can only be asked by someone who has no sense of what art is. It makes just as much sense to ask what the point is of staring in wonder at the beauty of the sun as it sets over the ocean. What's the point of inhaling deeply from a lush rose in late summer? What does that get you?

Art answers the question of purpose. Man is created for beauty and is only wholly human when he is allowed to serve it.

Creativity is written in the deepest DNA of man. Woe to a nation and woe to a life that no longer appreciates and loves art. Woe to a life that is no longer able to celebrate beauty for its own sake. Woe to a life that can no longer enjoy, and no longer play.

Where art is instrumentalized, it becomes mere craftsmanship or cheap advertising. Where art is no longer allowed to be for its own sake and follow its own rules, it becomes insipid and hollow.

The same thing happens with prayer, if it only serves some external purpose. Prayer helps us find stillness. Prayer powers our activities. Prayer brings blessing, maybe even the desired answer to prayer, and that is all true. But it's not everything!

Prayer is art. And for this reason, it is its own justification and does not need any other. Prayer is art. And for that reason, it lives from beauty and joy. Even the prophet Isaiah proclaimed that God would bring his people into his house of prayer and fill them with joy there (Isaiah 56:7): an eschatological fulfilment of that which God had always intended with the Temple, the place of encounter and the place of prayer. That is the prayer that God longs for: uninstrumentalized art, a free act of beauty for its own sake. Motivated by a free 'just because', and not by pressure.

STOKING THE FIRE

Often, I am asked what the correct form of prayer is. In my opinion there is no correct form of prayer. There is instead a variety of forms of prayer that fit different people at different stages of their spiritual lives. I do advise everyone to find *one* way that they then follow with a certain persistence. The practice of silence, Bible meditation, praise, liturgical prayer, consistent intercession, 24-hour prayer, Eucharistic adoration, reciting or singing passages from the Bible, listening prayer, the prayer of the Ignatian Spiritual Exercises, contemplative prayer, the Jesus prayer – all of these are forms that teach the intercessor something different.

I encourage you: enter the school of one or more of these 'artistic disciplines'. But don't expect immediately measurable results. Even the painter and the poet don't become masters of their craft in a few days. Send your heart on the journey of learning to pray – to become an artist, a master of prayer. Not immediately, but in the course of the coming decades. Don't be satisfied with anything less. You were created for God and our lives only find fulfilment in abandon to him, not tied to any utilitarian gain. In his own way every artist testifies to this truth, regardless of whether he is aware that it was God who engraved the word 'beauty' on the human heart or not.

THE KISS
Prayer in Love

SOMEWHERE ELSE ENTIRELY

In an aeroplane above New York, January 2012
When you're in love, you're usually lost in thought about your beloved. To be in love is a grace. It's not something you *do*. Sure, being in love is not everything. But a relationship in which the enchantment of the first love is permanently lost is one that has grown cold. When you're in love, you think only about the beloved day and night. The secret of day-and-night prayer is nothing other than the simple reality of being in love. This is the final and deepest secret of prayer …

I am sitting in an aeroplane but in my thoughts I'm somewhere else entirely. Below me are the lights of the big city; the yellow, orange and white points of light of Queens and Brooklyn stretch to the horizon, more of a sea than a city. Long, geometric lines that intersect, run parallel and away from each other; vast numbers of street lights along vast numbers of streets; amber haze above the endlessly repeating squares of neighbourhoods and, over to the right, the skyscrapers of Manhattan. Only the bluish light tracing the frame of each building is visible: cubic shapes, each lined up to the next, like Lego bricks. Think of all the cars, all the people! And above it all is the deep violet of the late evening sky, there where it touches the horizon, and the first couple of stars that appear in the indigo mist. My head is leaning against the small oval window. There is only the monotonous rumble of the engines and this view below me. But tears blur this spectacular sight. Because my heart is somewhere else entirely: there's a different scene before my inner eyes, a scene from the eighth chapter of the Gospel of John.

A FINGER IN THE SAND

Jerusalem, maybe AD *30*

She is lying in the dust. Her dark brown hair dishevelled, her face pushed down into the dirt. She is even more naked now, although she has hastily thrown on a robe. Even more naked than when she was caught in bed with him. Eyes that strip her. Eyes that pierce her. Eyes that kill her. 'Stone her!'

Hands had grabbed and pulled her. They had dragged her naked from the bed. Hands had pulled her hair. Hands had dragged her through town. Hands had thrown her to the ground and pushed her face into the dust. Hands that now gathered stones.

'Bring her to the rabbi, the adulteress!'

She lies in the dirt and the assembly of the righteous stands around her, looking down at her. There she lies.

There I lie. There lies my own wretchedness. There lies my own sinfulness. There I lie, handed over for judgement.

And there lies New York. There I sit and look down at a city of millions with all of its lights, all of its shine. The masquerade that is Times Square with all its flashing lights. This uber-city with all of its haste, its trouble, its evil, its pain and its dirt. The world-city. The city-world.

Moses commanded that she be stoned. She knows that she has earned death.

His feet are level with her eyes, in front of her in the dust. They had dragged her in front of the rabbi. What was he going to do? He, the very righteous one?

She is weighed down by her guilt. She shakes. She sweats. She is afraid. Not a single clear thought. Cowering. In the dust. Putting one and one together. What does it really feel like when they stone you?

It shouldn't have ended this way. It was just an affair. Waves of shame … she wants the earth to open up and swallow her before it can happen.

And now the questioning, the demanding, becomes increasingly bold. The bickering mob is now foaming at the mouth with indignation. 'What do you say?' She hears the voices clamouring above her. Her breathing is very shallow, but her chest is shaking. Her whole cowering body shakes soundlessly. Time stands still.

A murmur runs through the crowd, and suddenly air flows again around her temples. Somebody bends down. Her fists clench, her eyes shut even tighter. Is he going to grab me? Curse me? Beat me? 'Get away from me!'

But nobody grabs her. From the corner of her eye, through her tangled hair she sees him. It's the rabbi. He kneels next to her and writes. The men of the town are standing round the two of them. The righteous ones, the men with stones in their hands; all of them are watching the rabbi. But he does not return their looks. He has bent down, down into the sand of the street in which she is cowering. The sand she was clawing at with her fingers mere minutes ago. The sand on which her tears are falling now. Drop by drop the sand darkens beneath her face. The earth knows how she is suffering, and yet still won't swallow her up.

The rabbi is kneeling very close to her. She can almost feel his body. She hears the motion of his finger in the sand. He is writing, in the dust and the filth they had just dragged her through – through which they had dragged sin itself, in their minds. The deliberation of this gesture, the quiet composure of writing, creates a disturbing contrast to the still-raging crowd standing round them. What he's doing is incomprehensible. But now, since he is kneeling on the ground, at eye level to her, and not joining in with their condemnation, now, a bit of hope rises in her.

She struggles to hear what he says after he, so suddenly, picks her up. But all around them stones are dropped into the sand. Everyone is leaving, and no one is thinking about a stoning anymore. 'He who is without sin ...' Who said it? Without sin – who could be, ever? The stones are lying on the ground around them. The righteous dropped them in the sand, the sand which is wet with her tears. Her sand. Their sand. In which he wrote mysterious words that no one can read ...

And then he talks to her. Hesitantly, she raises her eyes, spying through matted locks, her face clotted with tears and dust. Had he really spoken to her? A few minutes ago, they were arguing about what to do to her – no one had actually questioned her. Now the rabbi is talking to her directly. He looks her in the eye and his gaze is soul-piercing.

Radiant. Gentle. Quiet. 'Neither do I condemn you,' are the words he says. Simple words. Unbelievable words. Words that stop time. These scandalous words that collapse the world around her and then rebuild it. These words …

These are the words that Jesus says again and again, even today. And they pierce me, right here on this United Airlines plane. 'Would I like another drink?' I almost don't hear the question, because my inner eye is fixed on her: on her, on the one Jesus looked at. On her, whose guilt is met by the perfectly free grace of Jesus. On her, for whom there is now no condemnation, ever since Jesus himself bent down next to her in the dust. Jesus, who let his life be shoved down into the dirt and didn't hold onto to it, unto death.

The free nature of Jesus' love lands on her and on the city below me, the city that embodies the world. This city with all its beauty, its suffering and its evil. The city that embodies me, too, just like the woman in the Gospel.

I lie there myself; I am accused by the voices inside me that recount my moral failings to me. And I know that they're right. I know that they are only agreeing with righteousness, with justice. Because someone who knows what an authentic life, saturated with love, looks like is confronted with the inescapable fact that his own heart makes a complete mockery of such aspirations.

And the sound of Jesus' fingers in the sand echoes again into this brokenness. The finger of the God who came to earth, and the sound of his words, 'Neither do I condemn you.' Exactly this grace, exactly this unconditional pardon, is what changes me. This unconditional acceptance is the only thing that can heal my heart at the deepest level, and free me to follow Jesus. The engines rumble and I weep. Under me lies New York.

THE GREATEST LOVE OF ALL TIME

That is the secret of life in love, and the secret of prayer in love: not that we first loved him, but he first loved us. Nothing sets our hearts as free as this simple, basic truth of the Gospel: you are loved. You are loved, and loved wholly and fully. The question of whether there is someone who loves us is the central question of mankind. Nearly every movie, nearly every book, contains this oldest and greatest theme: loving and being loved. In a large room packed full of strangers, where I feel uncomfortable, my feet will head, as if guided by an invisible hand, to the other end of that room if I know that someone who knows me and likes me is waiting there. There is no question whose telephone number I'm going to call if I have a car accident, receive a serious diagnosis or achieve some great success: I will call the number of someone who loves me. The feeling of being unloved drives people to suicide. The feeling of being ultimately, deeply and truly loved fills a person's life with purpose and joy. Those in love know this quite well! We are made for love. The love between husband and wife is an intoxicating beauty all by itself! And yet all human love, in all of its beauty, only reaches to a certain point in our hearts. Being in love does not last forever. No spouse will understand me in everything. No friend is there forever and ever. No mother's or father's love is so perfect that it never comes up against human limitations, never inflicts wounds. And yet we long for exactly that kind of love: for a love that always understands, stays with us forever and is even deeper than the God-given feast that is erotic love.

This is exactly the love that Jesus is talking about. It is exactly the love that the Gospel promises us. And it is the love that we only encounter if we radically experience that we were loved first. As long as the human heart continues to suspect that it is only loved in return for performance of some kind, it will not fully open. That's how people love. Even the best parents always love in connection with performance, good behaviour and conduct that meets expectations. That's how people are. But this is how we learn to be mistrustful, and we learn it fast. You love me? Where's the catch?

The overwhelming 'otherness' of the Gospel message that fundamentally and forever differentiates it from all world religions is the unconditional nature of the acceptance of God in Jesus Christ. While we were still God's enemies, he already loved us (Romans 5:10). *Enemies of God.* Once you understand this you no longer get easily distressed about your own wretchedness. You will be confronted by it in prayer, too. One is confronted by it in a life of following Jesus. But every disappointment at my own failure to perform can become an opportunity, an opportunity to lie in this dust one more time. To lie in the dust where his gaze met me for the first time, and where the adulteress heard his words for the first time. Where his words are heard even today by every person lying before him in the dust – everyone who capitulates and accepts his freely-given love. The love that proved itself on the cross, and in every drop of his blood that was spilled. A love that is open everywhere. Always. In New York. 3,000 metres above it. Or elsewhere.

A KISS BEFORE SPRING

Again and again, I have felt God's kiss: that sudden beam of light that is not of this world, the gentle touch of a gentle God. It was the same that day way back then, when I left my art teacher's class, and the magical realm of oil paints and organic forms, to walk through the late winter landscape to the semi-darkness of the abbey church in Metten. Once again there is the cool scent of incense and chalk. We are praying the Stations of the Cross, a contemplative act of devotion that follows the stations in Jesus' suffering. Jesus takes up the cross on his shoulders, falls, meets the weeping women, is nailed to the cross. I can't say why but it seems as if the curtain on these scenes of suffering is raised in the eyes of my heart. It's as if the story behind it were that of a great romance.

The romance story of an endlessly loving God, who does everything to bring his son's bride home ... through the hammer blows of the Roman executioners to the thin songs of the local church that dissipate in the nave, I think I can hear his own heartbeat. His heart that beats for me. As if transfixed, I stay there for more than an hour. Kneeling. Gazing. Swept away.

It was a kiss of love that March evening. And even though the buds on the trees were only just beginning to open in the fields after the brown of winter, there was the fragrance of blossom in my soul, as if it were summer and I had just fallen in love. As if the wounds of Jesus blossomed inside me into a bouquet of fresh roses. As if it were love that recounted itself and unfolded in this incomprehensible event, and not suffering. The love of a person who pays the ultimate price for love. The love of a God who is full of fiery determination. Love for ... me.

THE GREATEST LOVE STORY

The story of God with his people is a great love story: the story of a God who reveals his passionately burning heart, admittedly only gradually, and of a people who don't trust this love, who don't accept this invitation. And yet the trail is clearly evident. This gentle God only discloses his deepest secrets to his friends. But his offer of friendship is open to everyone who seeks him.

Even the very beginning of creation speaks of this encounter, of what it's all about. The second creation story expresses this in a fascinating way: every animal is created with a counterpart, and only Adam is placed alone by God in the Garden of Eden (Genesis 2:4–20). Man, created in the image of God, immediately senses the deficiency. He has no counterpart. He's alone. Why does God allow this search for a 'suitable helper for him'? Why does Adam even need to search for a suitable helper? Why does Adam have to name all the animals? Is it perhaps God's intention that Adam be a reflection of him in this respect, as well? To let him experience feelings that he has himself? The longing for a bride, the longing for an 'other', a partner, a *counterpart*? And God creates Eve out of the side of the sleeping Adam. Bone of his bone, flesh of his flesh. Adam, the primal image and precursor of the 'last Adam': that perfect man who was untouched by the Fall into sin, Jesus. Stories of the bridal quest are numerous in the Old Testament. In them, a servant is sent out, the bride is wooed with gifts. The search for a suitable bride is a perennial topic of Scripture, because it is an echo of the cry of God's heart. Where is my *counterpart*? Where is a people to whom I can open my heart? Where is my resting place? Where is a people in whose midst I can dwell and with whom I can speak face-to-face like with my friend Moses (Exodus 33:11)? The fundamental longing of the heart of God runs through all the laws and the, occasionally weird, archaic stories of the Pentateuch: Israel as his *counterpart*, as his friend. But again and again, refusal; again and again, falling away. And the prophets express, with ever greater clarity, what was already implicit: God is not just a partner in a covenant. He is not just King. He is not even just Father. His emotions are those of a bridegroom (Ezekiel 16), of a jealously loving, passionate, determined, wooing bridegroom who fights for the love of his bride.

This becomes abundantly clear in the book of Hosea. The young prophet is assigned by God to marry a prostitute and pay her to remain faithful to him. That is exactly how God loves his people … scandalous thought! A God who remains faithful to an unfaithful bride just because he is in love … but this is exactly the picture that the prophets paint. All of the threats of judgement and the fiery zeal of God – everything that hinders love – must be fought, and his people presented with an unavoidable decision. All this flows from the longing of God's heart: he wants to love and be loved. God feels. God is emotional. God is one who loves. Unfathomable mystery: the transcendent Lord of the universe loves. Is – *in love*.

This revelation reaches perfect clarity in Jesus. 'The bride belongs to the bridegroom', says John the Baptist (John 3:29). It is like a slogan over the public ministry of Jesus: Jesus as bridegroom. Again and again he himself speaks of a wedding banquet, of the return of the bridegroom. But who will his bride be? The Old Testament appears to end in broken pieces: the faithlessness of Israel – who will heal her? Will the last words be God's despairing cry, 'My people have forgotten me. Can a bride forget her jewellery?' (Jeremiah 2:32)? Eternally repeated human faithlessness, the virgin Israel become a whore, the covenant lying shattered in pieces. Where is renewal and purification supposed to come from? Who will be the bride?

Jesus is called the last Adam. He is the fulfilled, perfect Adam. And his match is his new Eve. Who will this be? No human being can become such a person through individual efforts. No legalistic obedience could change Israel at the heart level. But the heart is the only thing that matters to God. Who can make a heart of flesh out of a heart of stone? 'I will give you a new heart and put a new spirit in you; I will remove from you your heart of stone and give you a heart of flesh.' (Ezekiel 36:26). Man himself can never speak the word that will save him ...

It was God himself who created the bride from Adam's side. It will have to be a sovereign act of God that creates this new Eve, too. And this is the exact miracle that happens! It happens on Golgotha: 'Unless one is born of water and the Spirit, he cannot enter the kingdom of God.' Jesus said to Nicodemus (John 3:5 ESV). And it happens when water and blood issue from Jesus' side, when his heart is pierced by the spear. Water and blood, just like every birth. It happens when Jesus breathes out his spirit, because there are three who give witness: the water, the blood and spirit (1 John 5:8). And from the side of the new Adam who fell asleep on the cross, the new arises: the new creation. The Church. His *counterpart*. The bride. The bride for whom the divine bridegroom paid the bride-price of love. The price of that blood with which he bought us.

Under the cross: the beloved disciple who is now given as a son to Jesus' mother. That daughter of Israel who perfected Abraham's obedience by faith and gave an absolute 'yes' to God's plan for restoring Israel, and thereby saving the whole world. The beloved disciple adopted into the spiritual and natural family of Jesus.

The bride walks towards the return of her bridegroom. She has made herself beautiful and is adorned. This is the end of history: not a nuclear catastrophe and the end of the world, but the return of Jesus. The return of the bridegroom for whom the bride has made herself ready.

And this is precisely what prayer is. Prayer is the loving attentiveness of a bride in love. It is the longing of an inconsolably love-struck maiden. 'I will rise now and go about the city, in the streets and in the squares; I will seek him whom my soul loves', says the bride in the Song of Songs (Song of Songs 3:2 esv). The heart-cry of the intercessor is similar: 'Lord, I don't want to sit still. I want to arise. Even if it's at night. You who loved me first; you who rescued me from the filth and slavery of sin – you are worthy of being loved back. Because you kissed love awake in me. And this wound will not be healed. The world can no longer satisfy me. I will get up. I will be one of the wise virgins who approach the bridegroom, awake (Matthew 25:1–13), with the oil of love in my lamp and a fresh flame of prayer.'

And the day will come, when he comes. Many 'little days' will come. Because the intercessor who watches and waits, who seeks and knocks, will be given the gift of many such moments of the divine kiss. Admittedly, they aren't earned; they are a pure gift. But the God who said, 'Seek me' also said, you will 'find me!' (Jeremiah 29:13–14). Many little days will come when he will walk past softly. And a praying church will experience more and more days when he comes with power, and revival and miracles happen. All of that is a part of what the bride longs for. And yet her last yearning remains unfulfilled until the day when he comes in person to make all things new. Jesus will return. But he does not force this return on the world. God never overpowers his bride. But he is preparing her. Worldwide. He is preparing her through prayer. And unto prayer. Unto prayer in unity. Unto prayer that finally is fulfilled on the day when Jesus will return, visible as a bolt of lightning that starts in the east, and blazes across the sky to the west. He operates in agreement with, and will return for, a bride who calls out for him. 'The Spirit and the bride say: Come!' (Revelation 22:17).

STOKING THE FIRE

The study of the 'bridal' dimension of faith is an essential component of the history of spirituality in Christian mysticism. The beauty of it is that when one reads about the experiences of others, one is inspired by their hunger. It becomes yours. If you want to deepen your passion for Jesus, the bridegroom, get inspired by the works of great authors of the spiritual life. For me personally, these include Teresa of Avila, John of the Cross, Alphonsus Liguori as well as more recent authors like A.W. Tozer, Henri Nouwen or Thérèse of Lisieux.

It might be easier, however, to simply study the Scripture with a focus on this subject. There are many options for this: one can look for God's emotions specifically in every passage in the Bible. What emotion moved him to this or that pronouncement? The same applies in the Gospels: what is the emotional tenor in Jesus in that part of the narrative? The Baroque veneration of the 'Heart of Jesus' in Catholic piety refers exactly to this: access to the depths of Jesus' personality, which radiates in everything he said and did.

The basic idea is this: nothing will ignite your heart with love for Jesus as much as studying his love for us. Don't put any pressure on yourself. Love and passion are not anything you can condition yourself with, like doing push-ups. Feeling it immediately is not what it's about, either. Just take the Scriptures in your hand and read a chapter such as Isaiah 61, Psalm 45, Zephaniah 3. Moreover, whole books like the Song of Songs, Hosea, the Gospel of John or the Johannine Epistles are suitable for a study of this kind. But don't leave it at reading: start a conversation with the one whose feelings are described here. Ask him directly to ignite your heart with love for him. A prayer like that can sound like this:

Jesus, I thank you that you love me with an unending love. Thank you that you left the glory of your throne to take on human form.

Thank you that you went out to win yourself a bride.
Thank you that you paid the bride-price for me with your own blood.
Jesus, I want to accept your passionate love for me anew today.
Let me understand the depth of your love more, and ignite a love for you in my heart that burns ever brighter ... A love that cannot be extinguished through hardship or the dull force of the mundane.
Let this flame increase.
Draw me into prayer.
I want to know you and be fascinated by you.
Let the flame grow until the day that you return, or I stand before your throne of judgement.
Burning love in the heart of Jesus ... consume me!
Amen.

THE GAME

What I've Learned About Prayer from Children

A MESSAGE WRITTEN IN BLOOD

Pamucak, Turkey, June 2009

The New Testament is open in front of me. Yesterday we were at the place where he is buried: the Apostle John. There is only a simple tombstone, a flat slab amid high grass where once there had been a magnificent Byzantine Cathedral, marking the site where the beloved disciple of Jesus found his final resting place. Yet to me it seems as if I could feel his heartbeat here on this dried-up hill, where the wind carries the faint smell of the sea and the sounds of the village, here on the front edge of the green mountains. The heartbeat of him who heard Jesus' heartbeat on his last night. And he who, as ancient church history reports, composed the largest share of his writings right here in Ephesus.

I want to trace his steps, understand his message. So I sit on the beach for hours and read. I have undertaken to read, in Greek as much as possible, and pray through, all of John's writings. The reflection of the sun sinking in the west glitters before me like an ocean of gold coins. It is precisely the same sea that John saw. Did he think of a sea like this when he wrote of 'a sea of glass, clear as crystal' (Revelation 4:6), before the throne of God? But this time it is not the Revelation that stirs my interest but his letters. I read them over and over again. And it strikes me like lightning: he talks about love and almost nothing else. This is what love is, in this we recognize love, God is love, we remain in love if we love, and only the one who loves knows love and love, love, love ... he talks about love. A lot. Over and over. Why? Where does this fixation on this topic come from? What had he seen? What had he experienced that led to love apparently becoming his favourite subject? He was already a very old man when he wrote his letters, according to ancient chroniclers.

And his message seems to have coalesced more and more towards the end, 'We are loved, so let us love as well.'

But where does this focus on love come from? Why does John write about it constantly? Suddenly the realization hits me: of course he talks about love! Of course he talks about it more than Paul, Peter or James. He was there! He stood under the cross together with Jesus' mother, whom he then took into his family. He was there when Jesus' blood fell to the ground. And he was there when he died. And what is his testimony? What would a person recount who had seen this and what would he talk about? He talks about love. He talks about love, only, until his dying day, many decades later. 'This is how we know what love is: Jesus Christ laid down his life for us' (1 John 3:16).

It is about love. It's only about love. This simple, basic truth became jarringly clear to me on the beach of Pamucak. Prayer, too, is only about love. But what is love? And what does it look like? The whole world talks about love. But what is real love? John's answer is clear: you see it on the cross. You want to know what love is? Look at him. The true God who became true man, and let his royal blood pour out on the rock and dirt of Golgotha. Just so. For you and for me. That's how we know what love is.

The unavoidable fundamental demand of being Christian is this: 'since God so loved us, we also ought to love one another.' (1 John 4:11). And yet … how difficult it is to really love once one realizes what is really in us. How hard it is to faithfully, devotedly and truly love!

So, how do you learn to love?

Over the years I have grown in the conviction that love is not only the absolute core of the Christian life, but it's what prayer is about, too. If you can't love, you can't pray, either. Praying is loving. And learning to pray means learning to love. Where does this path begin, and what do its steep steps look like in our concrete prayer life? I am just now learning the first lessons of this great art, and to learn them I have to return to the school of children again and again.

LEARNING TO PLAY

Sukosan, Croatia, August 2013
So much that has happened in God's great story with us takes place in the small details. It's one year since my existential question about 'being' on the beach in France: it's summer again, and a year has passed in which I haven't thought about anything as much as about what it means to love, what it means to pray in spirit and in truth and what it means to encounter the other and myself in reality.

Once again I have sought out a place where I can pray in the morning. Once again I am staring out across the sea, even if the view is less spectacular. Once again I experience the virginal beginning of a dawning day. I try to be fully present before God, before myself. All at once, like a ripe apple falling into my lap, I decide that, today, I want to be fully present. Not just in my morning prayer time, although I especially need to be present when I pray; only there do I learn to catch my breath and not lose myself, to not miss God's presence in being. But it does not stop there. The small decision, but a major one for me, to just be there in these days on the beach. To be wholly present for my wife and my four children.

It doesn't feel special, starting the day this way. Nevertheless, the pink flowers on the side of the road seem pinker than before, the underbrush of thyme and bamboo seems thicker in the quiet of the Croatian morning. And then? The road to the baker. Breakfast in the loud, overflowing life of a young family. Playing card games. Reading stories, for hours. Paddling a rubber raft. Washing dishes. Reading another story. And quite consciously for these days: no media. No iPhone. No books, and no thought processes running in the back of my mind on how I could plan something major, or anything I really have to think through: just being there. Being there, with all the beauty of this abundant life and everything that gets on my nerves. Being there with my irritation, impatience and longing for everything that is not yet made whole.

This simple and self-evident attitude towards life seems almost strange. And yet I get tears in my eyes the next morning when I resume my place between the bushes. I sit there so quietly that not even a fox notices me; he stands beside me for a long time before bolting away. I get tears of gratitude for an imperfect, but abundant life; for the gift of my children and my wife; for the gift of a superabundance of overripe figs that we are allowed to harvest for free, and out of which we make marmalade, their seeds cracking between our teeth as we bite them. I get tears of gratitude for the gifts of earth, air and being. The relationship with my children, and my joy in them, becomes deeper in these days. How much I can learn from them! They were already where I want to go! They can play for hours, be happy with what is: they can be. Awed, thankful, sometimes angry and loud, but always authentic, always themselves. Romano Guardini calls the liturgy 'a holy game', and one could call prayer this, too. The thankful, open-handed attitude toward life that characterizes play is like the simplicity and joy into which God wants to increasingly free the intercessor. The beauty of play. The purpose-free character of pure being. Nowhere is this more visible than when we're praying, or when children are playing. The beauty of life that is ultimately a game that occurred to a loving God.

LEARNING TO LOVE

What is this last lesson in the travel diary of a man who set out to learn to pray? A small and yet immense lesson that will cost all who follow this path everything, and will not let them go for the rest of their lives. Praying means learning to love. And there is no love without attentiveness and being fully present. How little of this we see in our world! I listen to you but only with half an ear. I listen to you, but actually I already know what you're going to say. I listen to you, but in secret I am waiting on the pause in conversation so that I can tell my own (much more important) story. I listen to you, but really my mind is already made up. I listen, but I'm not really open to what you have to say. I listen, but in reality I'm not even there. At all. Not with my full attention, certainly. I'm there but only with my mind, and not with my heart or my emotions. I am not really listening. I'm really never completely there: a wasted life! Wasted chances for encounter and real relationships. Love that passed us by unnoticed. Because doesn't this important word, 'love', begin and end 'there'? Doesn't it begin and end there, where I let others be and accept them with thanks, just as he is, just as she is? Where I even just let him be, without understanding? Where I just let him have his secrets? Where I sacrifice my time and attention to give him space? Where I give my life, so that he can just be?

Prayer is like a time lapse and magnifying glass, imposed on the attitudes towards life that we half-consciously carry around with us. We carry this attitude all day long, are wholly unaware of it, exactly like a fish unaware of the water it's swimming in. In prayer the façades crumble. In prayer I am mercilessly confronted with my self-centeredness, with my useless daydreaming. Ultimately, I am confronted with my refusal to let go of myself, with my refusal to love. But real prayer lures me out of my spider hole; it invites me to perceive, to accept the truth. And in that, to accept God's truth: this truth that is greater than what I see and feel. To accept this God who is so much greater than my constructs. Accepting this Jesus whose word so effortlessly exposes the pettiness of my own heart, and who at the same time so warmly invites me not to just stay there but who invites me to the great game and the great love. Every hour of prayer is a collision and an invitation. A collision between the trivial things I consider important, and what he calls important. Jesus says to Martha how, 'Only one' thing is needed, and invites her to let go of her sterile buzz of activity (Luke 10:42). Not because working itself is bad, but because love grows cold if it doesn't leave space for what Mary does – sit at his feet and listen.

Being present and attentive: every relationship lives from this. Love lives from it. Life with God lives from it. Every hour of prayer is a collision and an invitation. An invitation ultimately to tell some story besides my own in my life. To sail somewhere, not just circling around my own priorities. Not seeing my own little continent. Prayer is sailing out onto a vast ocean beyond whose horizon an even vaster horizon opens into eternity. It is an invitation not to hold on to my own story but to let go of it and let it become part of the One Great Story. It is embarking into the new, endlessly vast story of the loving God who became human to choose a bride. A recipient for his love. To redeem this bride and teach her to love. And she becomes the one who awaits his return with burning lamps and a loving heart. This is the Great Story into which our little stories are woven. What an adventurous journey that such love joyfully invites our weak hearts to join in! Hearts in which a fire begins to burn that will never go out. A journey that brings weak and broken people to sing in the ruins of a darkened city. Day and night. With fire in their hearts.

Muddy
Pearl